COMPUTATIONAL MODELS
OF AMERICAN SPEECH

CSLI
Lecture Notes
Number 32

COMPUTATIONAL MODELS
OF AMERICAN SPEECH

M. Margaret Withgott and Francine R. Chen

CENTER FOR THE STUDY
OF LANGUAGE
AND INFORMATION

CSLI was founded early in 1983 by researchers from Stanford University, SRI International, and Xerox PARC to further research and development of integrated theories of language, information, and computation. CSLI headquarters and the publication offices are located at the Stanford site.

CSLI/SRI International **CSLI/Stanford** **CSLI/Xerox PARC**
333 Ravenswood Avenue   Ventura Hall   3333 Coyote Hill Road
Menlo Park, CA 94025   Stanford, CA 94305 Palo Alto, CA 94304

Library of Congress Cataloging-in-Publication Data
Withgott, Mary Margaret, 1954–
  Computational models of American speech / M. Margaret Withgott and Francine R. Chen
     p. cm. – (CSLI lecture notes ; no. 32)
     Includes bibliographical references (p.) and index.
     ISBN 0–937073–97–0.
     ISBN 0–937073–98–9 (pbk.)
     1. English language—Spoken English—United States—Data processing.
  2. Computational linguistics. I. Chen, Francine R., 1956–   . II. Title.
  III. Series.
  PE2808.5.W57 1993
  421′.54—dc20   92-45243
                                                             CIP

Contents

Preface

These studies were conducted as a part of an investigation into the difficulties due to variation in pronunciation, associated with the recognition of ordinary, fluent speech. Current recognition systems are limited either by reliance on a fixed vocabulary and restricted syntax or the requirement that the speaker pause briefly between words. While enormous progress has been made in this field, a deeper understanding of the kinds of variation exhibited by speakers has already suggested new ways of constructing the phonological models needed within successful systems.

Our studies explore American English pronunciation. This topic is of interest to speech engineers, linguists, and anyone who wishes to understand symbolic systems and communication. Analysis of the patterns and structures in large samples of speech elucidates our understanding of language, and is of practical benefit for speech technology. In the past, theorists and programmers have often relied on their own knowledge of a language or on extremely limited collections of transcriptions in investigations of pronunciation. Speech recognition researchers have taken the opposite tack, and have used large amounts of data for training systems; however, they have not, until recently, examined in much detail the information about pronunciation contained in the data. We have attempted to combine desirable properties from each approach by examining and developing probabilistic and rule-based computational models of transcription data using conditioning factors drawn from theory.

This monograph presents a perspective on phonetic variation as viewed through a series of computational models. We describe a computational system that applies low-level phonological rules to dictionary baseforms to generate sets of variant pronunciations. In addition to obvious applications, the system enables word similarity studies to be performed. We also describe a methodology for evaluating combinations of contextual descriptors. We then present a statistically-based technique to determine which factors account for specific phonetic alternations, and a method for automatically creating probabilistic pronunciation networks for speech recognition systems.

Which factors actually matter is not a question limited to the development of speech technology. Ontological issues have been central in twentieth century studies of phonetic variation. The existence of the syllable, for instance, has continued to remain a topic of debate to this day. Arguments, pro and con, have rested on theoretical premises which themselves form the topic of disagreement. In this work we hope we have contributed to the debate in a new way in the attempt to further the phonetic and computational practice of investigating how people speak. The computational models employ suprasegmental elements such as syllable boundaries, stress, and position in a unit called a metrical foot. Because all such units are controversial as part of descriptions of language behavior, finding that such factors are significant in modeling the data is of theoretical interest. At the same time such findings enable the creation of better models for both recognition and synthesis technology.

We are grateful to the many individuals who, in a variety of ways, made our work possible. In particular, we thank John Seely Brown, Allen Sears and Victor Zue. We wish to thank Aaron Halpern, Tad Hogg, Patti Price, Penni Sibun, Brian Smith and two anonymous reviewers for valuable comments on the manuscript. We also thank our many colleagues in the phonetics and speech communities for their interest and comments along the way, and those who have furthered this work either through direct collaboration or through sharing data and ideas with us. We particularly wish to acknowledge the collaboration of Steve Bagley in the work on the rule generation system described in Chapters 3–4, and Jeff Shrager in the work on decision tree induction described in Chapter 5. This research, conducted at the Xerox Palo Alto Research Center, was supported in part by the Defense Advanced Research Projects Agency. DARPA also sponsored the creation of the "TIMIT" (Texas Instruments (and) Massachusetts Institute of Technology) recordings and transcriptions which proved central to our work.

Francine Chen,
Meg Withgott,
Palo Alto, California

1

The enterprise of modeling the sound of a word

Computers are indispensable but our symbiosis with computers is not without problems. They are our partners for better or for worse. Also they are no better than the models that we employ. Models are necessary. Models can be intriguing, but models can also be deceptive, something that we often find when we confront models with the real world. (The role of speech research in the advance of speech technology, Fant 1990, p. 1.)

1.1 Computational models

Pronunciation speaks volumes about us, and that fact has never been adequately modeled by machine. Not only do we have little understanding of how attitude and meaning are conveyed in the speech waveform, we have limited knowledge about what is responsible for the subtle variations in the sound of vowels and consonants. Patterns of pronunciations in recorded speech are easy to see, but it is difficult to uncover the hidden factors that adequately predict the patterns. This work addresses the problem of modeling such hidden factors.

It should be said at the outset that our computational models make no attempt to uncover or display *why* someone pronounces a word in a certain way, whether because of social influences or physical reasons.[1] The sort of phenomena that we are considering concerns instead the likelihood of observing a particular sound sequence, and revealing ways to model that sound sequence. For example, given the American English speaking population as a whole, one is more likely to encounter 'tomato' with an "A" sound than "tomahto," and relatively unlikely to encounter "podato" for 'potato', but extremely likely to observe "ladder"

---

[1] For informative studies, the interested reader is referred to work on sociolinguistics (*e.g.*, Labov 1972) or to work on articulatory computer models, such as current work at Stanford University (Cooke 1990) or Haskins Laboratory.

for 'latter'. That such facts about pronunciation can be predicted, either by a person or by a machine, says something about the regularity of sound patterns in the language. A person may not always be able to introspect and give good reasons why such predictions seem natural; the merit of the computational models is that they make manifest (at least some of) the hidden conditioning factors that predict how words are pronounced.

The determination of which conditioning factors actually have predictive value aids the development of phonetic theory and leads to ways to improve speech technology. The selection of descriptive units is one fundamental question that we discuss in a historical overview in this chapter. We then turn to how a dynamic process, articulation, has been represented statically in scholarly works and computer programs. We review the debates regarding *symbol rewrite rules*, including rule ordering, rule application, and the association of probabilities with rule application. In the past, theorists and programmers have often relied on their own knowledge of a language or on extremely limited collections of transcriptions in investigations of pronunciation. Speech recognition researchers have taken the opposite tack, and have used large amounts of data for training systems but have not examined in much detail the information about pronunciation contained in the data. Also, simplifying assumptions are often embedded in the encoded pronunciation networks, such as eliminating phonological context or limiting context to the immediately adjacent sound. We have attempted to combine desirable properties from each approach by examining and developing models of the pronunciations found in transcription data of American English, using a rich variety of theoretically-motivated contextual descriptors. Beyond this work, as more databases become available to researchers, we can expect to see even more facts about pronunciation surface.

Two principal conclusions may be drawn from our work on computational models of American speech. The first is that it is possible to model differences in pronunciation using a good set of contextual descriptors without relying on hand-created rule ordering schemes. The second major conclusion is that "good" models of phonetic variation require the specification of very particular combinations of the contextual descriptors.

The differences in pronunciation are modeled with contextual descriptors that form just two basic categories:

1. sound *structure* and *composition*: (a) location and composition of the *phonetic element* in the linguistic structure (for instance,

TABLE 1.1
Conditioning Contextual Environments

CONTEXTUAL ENVIRONMENTS	INFORMATION USED
Structural position	word-initial/final foot-initial/final syllable-initial/final
Stress	unstressed syllable secondary stressed syllable stressed syllable
Precedence	following preceding preceding and following (intervocalic)
Segmental identities	consonant vowel named subsets of consonants and vowels
Morpheme type	specified lexical items function word content word

if it appears at the end of a syllable or at a word-boundary or if the structure is stressed); (b) the composition of previous and/or following sounds.

2. lexical *category*: that is, whether or not a phonetic element is in a *function word* (in a semi-closed class of lexical items that occur with high-frequency and that serve characteristic grammatical functions).

There are five major types of conditioning contextual environments that determine sound structure and composition (see Table 1.1). These environments are all independent and include information on word-edges, foot/syllable information, metrical stress, precedence relations, segmental identities (that is, the nature of individual phones), word identities, and morpheme type.

Using these contextual descriptors, we describe a computational system that creates the kind of variant pronunciations one observes in large collections of transcribed American speech. In addition to obvious technological applications, such as speech synthesis, the system enables word similarity studies to be performed that are more sophisticated than the use of Hamming distances sometimes found in psycholinguistic studies. We describe, too, a methodology for evaluating combinations of contextual descriptors.

The second conclusion is that the models require a tailored combination of contextual descriptors in order to capture phonetic regularities:

while phonological work makes this assumption, speech recognition models tend to employ uniform descriptive environments such as triphones (linear triples of phones), whole words, or environments such as the presence/absence of a word boundary throughout their data structures. We present a statistically-based technique to determine which factors account for specific phonetic alternations, and demonstrate a method for automatically creating probabilistic pronunciation networks for speech recognition systems.

The determination of which factors account for specific alternations is equally of theoretical interest. The existence of units such as syllables and feet, for instance, remains a topic of debate which is unlikely to be resolved on a purely theoretical basis. Our data-intensive methodology provides a complementary view of the extent to which a given factor accounts for the data at hand.

1.2 Historical note on studies of contextual variation

While people have carefully recorded facts about pronunciation since relatively early written history, only in the twentieth century has an extensive effort been made to write down phonological and phonetic descriptions of the full range of the world's languages. Yet while commercial applications and university chairs have materialized along with the study of phonology (the underlying structure of the sounds of spoken language), and the study of phonetics (the production and perception of speech), a field that encompasses both aspects of linguistic sound is still in the process of definition.

A general theory of linguistic information in speech signals was developed by phonologists and phoneticians in the early 1950's (Jakobson, Fant, and Halle 1952) based on the foundation provided by structuralism and the signal technology developed in the war years of the previous decade. It was an important effort to bring the observed capabilities of human listeners to the problem of speech science. In fact, the sophistication with which language data were analyzed, using intuition and theoretical models found useful in other linguistic domains, far surpassed the analysis of speech signals performed at that time. The signal classification systems were primarily viewed as a part of linguistic theory which nonetheless could prove useful for the machine recognition of careful speech (see Fant 1973, p. 143).

Given this early start, it is surprising that relatively few efforts have been made to consider theoretical units of structure while analyzing large corpora of phonetic productions. While a physicist, for instance, would not find the juxtaposition of theory and data to be out of the ordinary, the fact that this practice is somewhat unusual in phonology and speech science requires an explanation. We offer such an explanation with a very brief overview of the study of linguistic sound systems.

1.2.1 Units, the status of representations, and rules

The desire to understand the sound patterns of language was fueled early on by a wish, first, to see how languages were "genetically" related (that is, to trace common historical antecedents), second, to teach pronunciation, and finally, to conduct business in and teach in other languages. Only at the end of the nineteenth century did phonological theory emerge in a recognizably modern form.

Three themes in many variations can be discerned in this period: concern for the choice of descriptive unit; regard for the relationship between physical manifestations of a unit and the speaker's intent in producing it; and considerations concerning the expression of generalizations, including whether or not to employ transforming rule statements or multiple representations in describing sound variation.

1.2.2 Descriptive units

What is uniformly striking about descriptions until the 1960's is the tacit assumption that multiple units should be used by the analyst in investigating language. This assumption is one we return to in the computational work described in this book. In the early part of this century-long period, Baudouin de Courtenay and Ferdinand de Saussure, the Polish and Swiss precursors of what would become to be known as structural linguistics, both referred to *phonemes, syllables, morphemes, words, and word-groups*, phonological units still found in theories today. Baudouin also posited the existence of what is now termed *distinctive features* (his "kinemes/acousmemes") which describe the composition of theoretical entities such as phonemes. Baudouin and his student, Mikołaj Kruszewski, drew the distinction between morphologically-conditioned sound alternation and "phonetically"-conditioned alternation. They observed that some forms of phonetic alternation carry the potential to become morphologically significant (Baudouin 1972, p. 174), that is, that differences in meaning arise over time out of some sorts of variation in pronunciation. This observational sophistication was not always evident in the century to follow.

Most linguists who followed Saussure and Baudouin also made reference to both phonemes and "suprasegmental" units such as syllables.[2]

---

[2] A discussion of twentieth century phonological history is provided by Stephen Anderson (1985).

The latter were discussed either in terms of the distributional characteristics of the syllable (or, interestingly, as part of the identity of a segment, *e.g.*, Saussure's *coefficients soniques*), or in terms of prosodic units (*e.g.*, in the Prague School of Linguistics, Trubetzkoy's use of the syllable as a tonal domain). Along with phonological generalizations, the British Prosodic School formulated syllable-based generalizations to account for phonetic phenomena such as the patterning of stop releases. In the United States, Harris employed "long components" over several segments as a domain of phonological and morphological processes.

One of the most influential phonologists was the Moscow-born Slavicist and linguist Roman Jakobson who left Europe for the United States in the wake of the Second World War. He has written that his well-known theory of binary distinctive features arose out of analyzing prosodic units: "The difference between stressed/unstressed and long/short which I had to study in depth for my comparison of Czech and Russian verse directed my attention to the study of binary oppositions." (Jakobson and Pomorska 1983, p. 23). Perhaps ironically, the reducibility of units to primitive features later led phonologists to abandon prosodic units in descriptive work altogether. Jakobson himself wrote: "...the phoneme maintained its importance, but it changed from a primary unit to a derived one; that is to say into a combination of concurrent elements—just like the syllable, which is a derived unit in the temporal sequence of speech sounds." (Jakobson and Pomorska 1983, p. 26).

In what was to become known as generative phonology, it was a short step from derived units to their elimination. Noam Chomsky and Morris Halle defined a phonetic representation, *in toto*, as a "two-dimensional matrix in which rows stand for particular features; the columns stand for the consecutive segments of the utterance generated; and the entries in the matrix determine the status of each segment with respect to these features." (Chomsky and Halle 1968, p. 5). That this ultimate reduction led to bizarre formulations of syllable-based phenomena was noted by many (in particular, Kahn (Kahn 1976), especially as regards new predicates such as "weak clusters" (see Chomsky and Halle 1968, pp. 82, 103, 241)).

It did not help matters that phoneticians looked for, and did not find, convincing acoustic correlates of syllables. Not that they did not claim success: the Swedish phonetician Bertil Malmberg set out in the midfifties to dispel skepticism regarding the syllable through an experiment involving hand-painted, synthesized syllables. He wrote that he was reacting to:

...the opinion of those scholars who deny the existence of the syllable and/or of the syllabic frontier. Jespersen believed in the existence of the syllable but refuted the idea of fixed limits between the syllable...To Panconcelli-Calzia and von Essen, the syllable is only a psychological, traditional, or phonemic unit without any physical (acoustic or articulatory) counterpart. According to Panconcelli-Calzia, there are only larger or shorter groups of sounds, but no phonetically-delimited units within these groups...The reason for this negative attitude is of course the difficulty for phoneticians to discover, in the acoustic or physiological speech curves registered, any objective factor which could be interpreted as the physical counterpart of the distinction subjectively or linguistically utilized (Malmberg 1967, p. 294).

Malmberg literally painted consonant transitions either on leading or trailing edges of formants (bands of resonant energy visible in a Fourier transform of the speech waveform), and playing back the result, asked subjects if the consonant belonged to the first (trailing) or second (leading) vowel. The subjects performed perfectly when there was a sizable (200 millisecond) gap between the vowels and they performed at less than chance when the gap was at 20 milliseconds. Malmberg then concluded that "...for the first time, a possible physical basis for the syllabic division has been found" (Malmberg 1967, p. 300).

Malmberg's mixed experimental results can be explained in part by subsequent perceptual work by Pisoni (1977) and Massaro (1972). Pisoni showed that the temporal resolution of the auditory system is coarser than 20 milliseconds in identifying onsets of two sounds separated both temporally and in frequency, thus accounting for Malmberg's subjects' behavior when they encountered the shorter gaps. Similarly, Massaro demonstrated that significant temporal masking occurs when a silence gap is less than 40 milliseconds. To try to draw a conclusion, one may learn about phonetic syllable divisions in slow speech, but in fast speech, it seems unlikely that low-level perception is adept at interpreting this sort of syllable boundary.

In the United States at least, the syllable was not fully reinstated in phonological theory until the mid-seventies, and its status remains nebulous in speech technology, where it is possible to find units such as demisyllables and diphones. These make the task of artificially synthesizing language simpler, but do not seem to play a convincing role in describing linguistic sound patterns. In the seventies, Liberman and Prince (1977), Kahn (1976), and Kiparsky (1979) all employed suprasegmental units in their analyses of English. This phonological work formed the framework for linking prosodic units with allophonic phenomena in contemporary research. In this and related work, the metrical foot, a stress group containing at least one syllable, was reintroduced into the mainstream. Other traditional units, such as the brief timing unit known as the *mora*, similarly have reappeared in American linguistics. While units such as the foot never disappeared from the British phonological scene, in the United States, respect for information theory and general mathematical simplicity obscured the intuition that linguists had had, since at least the time of Panini (*circa* 300 B.C.), that sounds are metrically grouped in language.

While the stand was made that such metrical units function in a non-metrical setting, and that the sub-units of the syllable (the onset, nucleus or peak, and coda) were *bona fide* linguistic entities, the relationship between such units and phonetic realizations remained unclear. Over the decade, phonological evidence was amassed from a variety of languages. Much of the evidence, however, only related either to stress systems or to phoneme distribution patterns.[3] In later chapters we look at phonetic patterns correlated with metrical units, not unlike the older British practice.

Part of the difficulty in comparing views regarding phonetic representation is the lack of consensus on what is phonetic and what is *allophonic*. Even the vocabulary is not quite straightforward. Explaining popular usage in phonetics, Ladefoged (1975, pp. 35–36) writes:

> When we transcribe a word in a way that shows none of the details of the pronunciation that are predictable by phonological rules, we are making a **phonological transcription**. The phonemic segments are usually placed between slanting lines. Thus we may say that the underlying phonemic segments in "cat" and "catty" are /kæt/ and /kæti/. But the phonetic segments that are actually pronounced are usually [kæt] and [kædi].
>
> The variants of the phonemes that occur in detailed phonetic transcriptions are known as **allophones**. They are generated as a result of applying the phonological rules to the segments in the underlying forms of words.

In this quote, and throughout our writing, the term *segment* is used loosely or simply pre-theoretically. Like the term "object" in the vision literature, what one conceives of as being a segment is contextually dependent. A segment rarely stands in one-to-one correspondence to a phoneme. In fact, in most current phonological theory, what once was commonly called the phoneme is now often thought of as a composite structure, reflecting a move away from viewing abstract sound units as

---

[3]Halle and Kenstowicz (1991, p. 457) recently wrote: "One of the most important concepts to emerge from the phonological theory of the past ten to fifteen years has been metrical constituency. The constituency has no direct or uniform phonetic correlates. It can only be detected indirectly through its effects on phonological rules and constraints..."

discrete, noncompositional entities. By the same token, discussions of allophones are now discussions concerning *features*. When the older vocabulary is still used, the term 'allophone' is used as a characterization of sounds that do not distinguish lexical items but that form a record of differing ways to pronounce words. The terms still have currency in speech recognition literature with the usage Ladefoged describes. For clarity, we adopt the term *dictionary symbol* to refer to the characters transcribed in a pronunciation dictionary, even though the word 'phoneme' might be employed in work similar to ours. In the general speech literature, the term *phone* is used interchangeably with *speech sound*, and can refer to allophones, models of acoustically similar regions in a speech waveform, or to the registration of a perceptual event. In the speech recognition literature, a phone may even be a stop burst, but it will never be a "deleted variant" [∅], in the tradition of allophonic description. Because of the wide range of referents this term has acquired, we have chosen to adopt the more neutral term *phonetic element* in this work to refer to what is denoted by low-level phonetic transcription symbols.

Linguists have always recorded phone variants; it has proven impossible to agree on the appropriate degree of detail to represent. What is phonetic and what is phonological is under active investigation. For instance, Peet (1988) notes that low-level palatalization caused by a glide [y] (as in "did you" → [dij(y)u]) differs from that caused by a fricative [š] (*e.g.*, "gas shortage"). Although often collapsed as a single phonological rule (see Halle and Mohanan 1985), these two kinds of palatalization exhibit asymmetries in terms of direction of assimilation, assimilation of voicing, and sensitivity to prosodic conditioning factors. Palatalization of stops is possibly best described as a gradient phonetic rule which exhibits a greater degree of partial assimilation, while palatalization of fricatives shows more categorial phonological attributes.

A final problem in defining what is phonetic arises from the fact that phonetic realizations are highly variable. Labov and other sociolinguists have been successful in demonstrating that some of the variability correlates statistically with social circumstances. Yet perhaps this work has only added to the sense that phonetic variation is something far removed from phonological description.

Our work shows that low-level phonetic variation also correlates with linguistic structure such as the syllable. This has been difficult to demonstrate convincingly in the past with the limited data researchers have had access to. New data have permitted us to quantify the relationship between abstract, linguistic representation and perceived differences in language sound. This means that we can add more content to the notion of a sound being "predictable" given "an environment," and it means that we have developed a methodology that will allow phonetic patterns across languages to be compared.[4]

1.2.3 The idea of rules and networks

In Chapter 3 we will model phonetic regularities observed in transcribed speech data in the form of *rules*. Noam Chomsky spearheaded modern work on rule formalisms and formal language theory, although he tends to downplay this work himself.[5] His efforts have been taken advantage of not only in natural language work, but also in general computer science areas such as compiler design, in the same fundamental way that work in mathematical logic is now used routinely for VLSI. In linguistic studies, generalizations are frequently stated in the form of rules. For instance, the fact that the final [k] in *electric* corresponds to an [s]-sound in *electricity* can be expressed axiomatically, correctly excluding cases such as when the final [k] in *mimic* remains as such in *mimicking*. In this way, a phonological grammar can be looked at as describing the infinite string set of a language.

Rules continue to be an important topic of inquiry. In the past few years, a trend materialized that has favored computational architectures without, at least, explicit rules (*e.g.*, Rumelhart and McClelland 1986). This research program has been subject to several lines of criticism, however, both for the impossibility of modeling certain kinds of behavior and for predicting phenomena that do not occur in natural language (see, for instance, the critique by Pinker and Prince (1988)). More recently, connectionist architectures have been designed which reinstate rules (Touretzky 1989; McMillan, Mozer, and Smolensky 1991), and a clearer understanding of rule and partial rule-like behavior appears to be emerging.

In evaluating rule-based phonological grammars, there are at least six agreed-upon considerations: (a) the generality and extensibility of the posited rule (is it common in other languages?); (b) the number of levels of representations that are posited; (c) the form of the representations; (d) accuracy and coverage; (e) simplicity; (f) the sort of rule ordering is employed. Each of these considerations is complex. While we will touch on them all eventually, we will discuss rule ordering in most detail.

---

[4]Anderson (1985, p. 266) argues that the demonstration that an acoustic pattern is linguistically significant hinges on systematic differences across languages: "There is a principled basis for positing a level of representation of utterances which is neither a complete physical record nor confined to the distinctive features of the language in question. This is exactly a phonetic representation in the traditional sense."

[5]Several pioneering formal language articles are conveniently collected in Luce, Bush, and Galanter 1965.

1.2.4   Rule ordering

The rule *component* we will be concerned with in Chapter 3 can be thought of as an optional, or stylistic, addition to a process that takes an abstract, phonological string from a dictionary and outputs pronounceable, phonetic transcriptions. We can say that this component "follows" the pronounceability process; that is, the variant pronunciations we are concerned with are related to the pronounceable forms and not to the abstract dictionary entries. In terms of generation, considering the component "after" the dictionary constitutes a weak form of rule ordering. The component itself has no rule ordering. However, the component can be rerun several times (until no new pronunciations are generated), so it is preferable to think of such rules as applying in all possible orders. In Chapter 5 we produce probabilistic finite state networks that relate dictionary forms to surface forms. Again, these do not exhibit rule ordering.

Rule ordering is implicit in some early twentieth century work, and much has been made of this in later generative critiques. The ubiquitous type of rule ordering is what Kiparsky termed the 'feeding' order. A feeding relation between two rules exists where rule β applies to the output of rule α, instead of to the base string. Some linguists only permit feeding orders, others describe general feeding orders but make allowances for exceptions. Chomsky and Halle exploited rule ordering to the limit: while rule ordering had been used extensively before (including in their own linguistic work), Chomsky and Halle formalized the practice and simultaneously initiated a heated decade-long debate.

At issue was whether or not rule ordering could go beyond feeding orders; that is, whether or not rules could apply simultaneously, or if by permitting certain orders, applications of later rules could be selectively blocked, or if rules could apply first to the innermost part of a word and then work out to affixes, or whether any statement regarding application should be allowed at all. A few linguists, too, sought out general principles that would eliminate the need for statements regarding particular rule orders yet preserve the capacity engendered by ordering rules (*e.g.*, Kiparsky 1968; Koutsoudas, Sanders and Noll 1974).

Since phonological forms were viewed in this decade as rows and columns manipulated as strings, not much emphasis was placed on the kinds of structural descriptions assigned to the strings, even for suprasegmental phenomena such as stress. Rule ordering was frequently invoked in cases where a statement that made reference to syllabic structure may have sufficed. For instance, Kisseberth (1973) presents many examples as evidence either for explicit rule ordering or for so-called global rules that have access to the details of the derivational history of the word (the input and output of previous rule applications). Without claiming to offer an actual analysis based on a careful examination of the language, we can sketch a syllable-based alternative to a typical case, such as the one cited by Kisseberth for the language Sea Dayak:

> A vowel is nasalized if preceded by a nasal...; *mãta* 'an eye', *gonẽ* 'a sack', *mõã* 'the face'. The rule is inhibited, however, by the presence of a consonant between the nasal and the vowel (actually there appear to be some glides which do not block nasalization, but this point can be ignored here); thus *nãỹã?* 'straighten' as opposed to *nãŋga?* 'to set up a ladder'. A word such as *nãŋga?* has an alternate pronunciation where the voiced stop following the nasal consonant is omitted: *nãỹa?* (Kisseberth 1973, p. 428).

The point of this kind of example is that although a sound (the [g]) is deleted, exposing another sound to potential modification (in this case leaving the [a] next to the nasal engma "ng"), the exposed sound does not undergo the expected modification; here, the [a] does not nasalize. One would have to study the language carefully in order to offer actual phonological rules for the language, but it seems reasonable to consider a syllable-based analysis (particularly in light of the parenthetical remark regarding glides). If engma is a true phonetic element in Sea Dayak (that is, if it is not a pre-nasalized /g/ stop), we could imagine the following derivations, where the domain provided by the syllable enables us to distinguish two cases without the use of rule-ordering:

(1)   Pseudo-Sea Dayak

naŋa?	naŋga?	baseforms without nasalized vowels
[na][ŋa?]	[naŋ][ga?]	putative syllable structure
[na][ŋa?]	[naŋ][a?]	/g/-deletion
[nã][ŋã?]	[nãŋ][a?]	nasalization within syllable

'straighten' 'set up a ladder' *gloss*

As Kahn (1976) remarked, many phonological processes seem to be sensitive to syllable structure. Certain of these processes are low-level alternations in "sentence-level" or *postlexical phonology* (Mohanan 1982; Kiparsky 1981). It may be that, for instance, explicit rule ordering statements are enlightening for the description of a language's morphophonology, with its attendant historical idiosyncrasies, but obscure lower-level phenomena, once prosodic structure is factored into the equation. Viewed in this light, it is not so surprising that David Stampe proposed simple iterative feeding orders, given his principle focus on low-level rules (or "processes" in his theory).[6] He claims that

---

[6]Cf. also Koutsoudas' 1976 random sequential hypothesis.

rules can reapply if their structural description is met, and that processes of syllabification and segment deletion, insertion or alternation can trigger changes in the structural description. His examples show, he writes, that:

... so-called 'feeding order' is an iterative sequential application of processes in random order, no order at all. The derivation terminates when all applicable processes (plus or minus optional ones) have applied (Stampe 1973, p. 66).

When hundreds of low-level rules are collected for a language, the task of evaluating a claim such as Stampe's (or any rule-ordering claim) becomes nearly intractable using the traditional tools of the phonologist. Rule interactions are complex, and each new word, so long as it has a distinct baseform, has a new derivation consisting of various interactions among subsets of rules. But computers stand in contrast to people with paper and pencil, since they are good at just this kind of mechanical rule application over large amounts of data. In Chapter 3 we explore some consequences of a position similar to Stampe's and look at the viability of allowing only iterative feeding orders through constructing large rule components and applying them iteratively over large sets of words. The conclusion is that the emphasis of research on low-level rules should be on rule predicates—what the rules talk about—and not on ordering.

1.2.5 Probabilities

In the phrase 'cat in', the /t/ may be flapped, glottalized, aspirated, or unaspirated. However, it is possible to do more than to predict what sequence of phonetic elements may be pronounced—the relative frequency or probability of a phonetic element in a given context can also be identified. In our 'cat in' example, we can say, in rough terms, that the /t/ is seldom aspirated and often flapped. Quantification of such information is useful to speech recognition systems for building word models, as well as being potentially useful to speech synthesis systems for adding variability for more natural sounding speech.

Early recognition systems, such as those based on template matching and the network-based Harpy system (Lowerre 1976), relied primarily on spectral matching for scoring. In 1975, the DRAGON system introduced the idea of a stochastic model, commonly called a *hidden Markov model*,[7]

---

[7]A hidden Markov model is a doubly stochastic model commonly used in speech recognition. It may be thought of as an finite state machine which is enhanced with transition probabilities on the edges, or arcs, and a probability score indicating the quality of match between the model and data to be recognized at each node. (For an introduction to Hidden Markov Modeling, see Rabiner and Juang 1986 or Poritz 1988.)

(HMM) to speech recognition (Baker 1975). Although the ideas from the DRAGON system were generally slow to catch on, most current speech recognition systems, such as the IBM Tangora system (Jelinek 1985) and the Carnegie-Mellon SPHINX system (Lee *et al.* 1989) are now based on those ideas. By scoring candidates with statistically-based costs, the performance of recognition systems improves.

In present speech recognition systems, pronunciations of words are often modeled using pronunciation networks which represent alternative pronunciations in a compact form. These networks are derived either by hand or by application of hand-derived phonological rules (following, *e.g.*, Cohen and Mercer 1975; also see Cohen 1989). Probabilities of sequences of phones are then assigned by training using the Baum-Welch reestimation formulas (see Baum *et al.*, 1970, Levinson, Rabiner and Sondhi 1983; Rabiner and Juang 1986), as in SRI International's (henceforth, SRI) DECIPHER system (Weintraub *et al.* 1989). However, speech networks do not have to be hand-crafted if sophisticated clustering methods are used, and appropriate contextual descriptors, including metrical units, are incorporated. In Chapter 5 we show that with knowledge of such contextual descriptions for allophonic variation, and machine learning procedures, such networks can be created automatically.

1.2.6 Concluding remarks

Three largely disjoint communities have developed models of variability in pronunciation. One is the speech recognition community, which has invested considerable effort in creating word models in the form of pronunciation networks. A second community comprises theoretical phonology, with researchers who have investigated representational issues regarding pronunciation (including the question of rule application), and studied structurally-based contextual factors that correlate with variation. Third, sociolinguists have formulated probabilistic models of variation based on cultural factors.

In our work, we have developed a number of computational models that explore the use of structurally-based contextual factors. We also devise probabilistic models, using such factors, which have been automatically converted for use in recognition systems. In later chapters we describe the way we have incorporated theoretically and empirically-motivated contextual descriptions into a computational system that discovers regularities in American speech.

In these ways, we have combined the insights and interests of at least two of the research communities that explore variability in speech, phonology and speech recognition. At some point, it would be advantageous to connect our metrically-based computational models to sociolinguistic models of an individual's speech, but unfortunately it will not be accomplished in this monograph. The data used in our studies, method of collection and method of transcription will be discussed in the next chapter.

2

Hand-transcribed American English speech

The investigator must take care to secure natural, unguarded responses. Slow and emphatic utterance differs from normal speech, especially in the treatment of syllables usually weak. For this reason the interview should be carried on as far as possible in the form of a conversation. If the desired expression is first uttered in isolation, the informant should be led or directed to utter it in context, under normal stress and at the usual speed. A question such as: 'How would you say it if you were talking to your wife or a neighbor?' often sets the informant right. (Instructions for Field Work, Kurath 1939, p. 48.)

It is possible to begin the process of modeling speech by drawing explicitly on theoretical phonological constructs. Such theoretical entities, however, are themselves arrived at in a way that would no doubt alarm speech engineers. Developing phonological theory is more reminiscent of the way, say, law is taught at Harvard than anything resembling the way data are examined using techniques such as clustering or analysis of variance. Famous cases are analyzed, dissected, reanalyzed and, over the course of many years, there emerges a feel for both the subject matter and approaches to it. It is this wealth of diversity in the analysis that makes phonological theory an interesting point of departure. But then, moving from phonology to the domain of phonetics is a little like bringing a law practice to a foreign country—some of the principles and broad outlines remain intact, but the details are bound to be new and surprising.

In order to test a set of theoretical constructs in modeling the pronunciation of a word, a reasonable sample of the possible pronunciations is required so that meaningful patterns in the sample may surface. One of the ways to sample conversation is by analyzing transcribed speech. A transcription of what a native speaker has said is recorded by someone trained in perceiving and writing down those phonetic distinctions that a specially-designed notation supports. For purposes of modeling phonetic phenomena, a very large sample of highly detailed, accurately transcribed data is required. While it is relatively straightforward to build computational models of morphophonological phenomena, such as producing the dictionary pronunciation of 'electricity' given a baseform 'electric', it is another matter to model how that pronunciation actually sounds. Even primitive data collection methods will yield a set of correspondences between our dictionary pronunciation and observed pronunciations contained in recordings; more sophisticated methods are needed to uncover the environments in which such correspondences hold.

Analyzing the patterns involves more than simply noting the *mappings*, or correspondences, between observed pronunciations and a *dictionary baseform* listing of the pronunciation, because mappings are constrained by multiple factors. In developing our models we have found that important factors depend on sound *structure* and *composition* (such as the location and composition of the phonetic element, and its place in a relational prosodic structure), and second, lexical *category* (whether or not a phonetic element is in a function word). Sound structure and composition are central concepts in all phonological theory, although different theories describe structure in different ways. Theoretical constructs such as syllables and function words are useful as candidate factors in the computational modeling of speech.

2.1 The TIMIT database

Texas Instruments demonstrated the value of speech databases[1] with the creation of a large set of recordings of the digits 0-9 spoken by a diverse set of American speakers (Leonard 1984). Such databases are useful for training and evaluating automatic speech recognizers even if they are supplied with only orthographic (as opposed to phonetic) transcriptions. With phonetic transcriptions, they become useful for developing phonetically-based recognition systems, and for studying general speech behavior for a variety of purposes.

In 1985, DARPA-supported[2] speech researchers decided to mount an

---

[1]The term 'speech database' can prove confusing. A speech database is simply an organized collection of (usually digital) signal data, orthographically or phonetically transcribed. It is often divided into training and testing portions, with speaker identity, dialect, and other keys associated with each utterance.

[2]DARPA stands for the Defense Advanced Research Projects Agency. DARPA is a government agency and is the most significant single source of funding for research on computer science and speech technology in the U.S.A.

effort to collect and transcribe a new speech database named TIMIT (a concatenation of TI and MIT, the two organizations who were the key developers). The goal, as stated in Lamel, Kassel, and Seneff 1986) was ambitious:

> A complete database should include different styles of speech, such as isolated words, sentences and paragraphs read aloud, and conversational speech. The speech samples should be gathered from many speakers (at least several hundred) of varying ages, both male and female, with a good representation of the major regional dialects of American English (Lamel, Kassel, and Seneff 1986, p. 1.)

This goal was achieved to a large extent. In December 1988, NIST, the National Institute of Standards and Technology, released a compact disk of the DARPA TIMIT Database which contained 4200 sentences produced by 420 speakers.

This database could be faulted on several grounds, most notably in the collection of the data, since speakers were asked to read sentences instead of speaking spontaneously. However, as of this writing, it remains one of the most useful and widely used American English databases. Also, despite the fact that the sentences are read, many of the speakers sound remarkably casual. Other speakers sound stilted, and while their productions may be less interesting for studying certain types of phonological phenomena, the sheer volume of the data permits a reasonable look at many speech processes.

In constructing the TIMIT database, Texas Instruments performed the task of recording speakers from many parts of the country (Fisher *et al.* 1987). The original digital tapes were recorded using both a Sennheiser close-talking microphone and a pressure sensitive microphone at 20kHz. NIST downsampled the tapes to 16kHz for redistribution to the DARPA speech community.

MIT undertook the task of transcribing the tapes. The method of transcription was more sophisticated than most such efforts. In the transcription project, multiple parametric representations of the speech utterance, along with the original waveform, are displayed on a Symbolics Lisp workstation using the *Spire* facility developed by Shipman, Zue, and several graduate students in the Research Laboratory for Electronics at MIT. The transcriber listens to the tape over headphones and enters a transcription using a sixty-character alphabet (including silences). Difficult portions of the tape can be simultaneously viewed and replayed in a loop. When the transcriber is satisfied with the phonetic character string, an automatic alignment program associates the symbols with time intervals in the signal (Leung and Zue 1984).

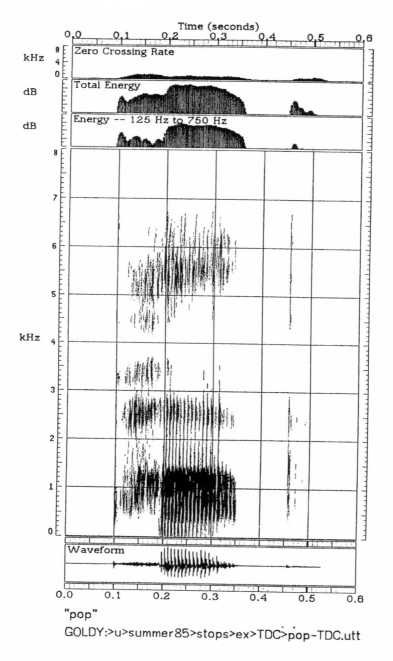

FIGURE 2.1   MIT's transcription environment for the TIMIT tapes

The alignment is then hand-adjusted, if necessary. Figure 2.1 shows a screen image of the MIT transcription environment. We think that first listening to the speech, and then visually examining a spectral representation of it is a good way of overcoming one's own dialect biases when transcribing.

MIT also designed a portion of the sentences that the subjects read, which contained phonetically rich contextual environments for inducing phonetic variation. These were the sentences we chose to use. TI contributed other sentences intended to round out the representative sound environments in American English. SRI added to the set with two sentences meant to draw forth dialect differences among the subjects. These sentences were: 'She had your dark suit in greasy wash water all year'; and 'Don't ask me to carry an oily rag like that'. In our statistical analyses we eliminated the "dialect" sentences. Because each speaker read the same sentences, using these data would have skewed the distribution of the contextual factors we were interested in.

2.1.1 Use and augmentation of the TIMIT data

In most of the experiments we employed the 450 sentence types designed by MIT. The transcriptions provided us only with phonetic character strings for each signal. Stress was not marked, nor was any tonal representation attempted. Duration of the transcribed symbols was directly computable, however.

We augmented the data with word boundaries, syllable and foot boundaries, and indications of primary and secondary stress (and the absence of lexical stress), and added the lexical representations to an online dictionary we developed called the *X-dictionary*. These augmentations were viewed as underlying properties of each lexical item, and not features of the acoustic signal. We did not mark emphasis or contrastive stress. It should be added that syllable boundaries were recomputed as phonetic elements were deleted and inserted in the model of the Pronunciation Prediction System (PPS) described in Chapter 3.

In all our experimental work we made use of *mappings* between dictionary entries (phonological transcriptions) and phonetically transcribed strings. The mappings are simply the symbol-to-symbol correspondence between the dictionary and transcription strings, leaving aside the conditioning contextual predicates that describe the correspondence. *Rules*, as introduced in Section 1.2 in the previous chapter, employ such predicates.

As noted above, we refer to the symbols in a pronunciation dictionary simply as *dictionary symbols* and not as phonemes, which is at odds with speech recognition practice. A dictionary symbol may represent several variant pronunciations. For example, the dictionary symbol /t/ is associated with the pronunciations including the aspirated, flapped, and unreleased variants that characteristically occur in 'tap', 'butter', and 'pat new', respectively.

Mappings from the dictionary symbols to a phonetic level of representation were derived automatically by comparing transcriptions of spoken speech with a phonological transcription of the words spoken. Transcriptions from the X-dictionary formed the dictionary symbols; hand-transcribed segments from the MIT sentences (referred to as the "sx" sentences) form the transcription strings the TIMIT developers call *phones*. Following speech recognition practice, this is largely, but not entirely, an acoustic notion. For example, in the TIMIT database, an aspirated plosive which exhibits a closure, such as a [pʰ] pronounced with a silent period while the lips are closed, is labeled as a closure segment followed by a separate aspirated segment. This produces a labeling suitable for a speech recognition system, since the closure and release are acoustically distinct.

Since our primary interest is the type of variant observed, our alignment procedure replaces the two TIMIT phones corresponding to a closure plus release with a single element we refer to as a phonetic element, representing the aspirated plosive. For sounds which do not represent more than one acoustically distinct segment, the phonetic element and the TIMIT phone representation are identical. In addition, both the TIMIT phones and phonetic elements are used to indicate epenthesis, as when *warmth* /wɔrmθ/ is pronounced with an unreleased [p] as [wɔrmp⁻θ].

The computed mappings and the associated dictionary context of each mapping were entered into a database for several studies. Various forms of contextual information were explored. The use of the mappings will be discussed in detail in Chapters 3 and 5.

2.2 Symbols used in displaying phonological transcriptions

Table 2.1 presents how vowels are rendered in the text, and also how they appear more compactly in dictionaries. To this list we can add the vocalic sound in American English that involves retraction of the tongue and narrowing of the pharynx, transcribed as a syllabic r [r̩] (as in 'earn'); other syllabics including [n̩] (as in 'button'), [l̩] (as in 'apple'), [m̩] (as in 'impress' with initial vowel deletion); and the diphthongs [aʷ] (as in 'how'), [aʸ] (as in 'why'), and [oʸ] (as in 'toy'). It should be noted

TABLE 2.1
Vowel Symbols

	FRONT	CENTRAL	BACK
HIGH	i as in *seat* I as in *sit*	ɨ (barred-i, —) as in *seat**e**d*	u as in *suit* ʊ as in *soot*
MID	e as in *sate* ε (eh, E) as in *set*	ə (schwa, or x) as in *s**a**tirical* ʌ ("stressed schwa")	o as in *so*
LOW	æ (or @) as in *sat*	a as in *sod*	ɔ (open-o or c) as in *saw*

Additional symbols include the diphthongs: [aʷ] (W), [aʸ] (Y), and [oʸ] (O).

that the simple tense vowels of English are often in actuality somewhat diphthongized, so that [i], [e], [o], [u] could as well be represented as [i⁽ʸ⁾], [eʸ], [oʷ], (and very rarely) [uʷ].

The consonant symbols commonly used in this monograph appear in Table 2.2, along with the names of their articulatory classes and the alternate ASCII version symbols used in the dictionaries. These are the phonological symbols used in our computational models.

2.3 A short primer on American speech

The most valuable feature of the TIMIT database is its documentation of variation in American speech. Most Americans can usually identify the speech of another American, and often as belonging to a particular geographically- or ethnically-defined dialect. No one knows how many distinct dialects of American English there are, or how to draw clear dialect boundaries across socio-economic borders. Yet the collection of these diverse ways of speaking constitutes American English. Someone, say, a telephone operator, who speaks with Americans with a broad range of dialects must and can internalize quite flexible models of vowels, consonants, and changes to them in order to understand American English. Mere mappings, or correspondences between observed pronunciations and dictionary baseforms, do not suffice for understanding the kind of variation any native speaker is capable of creating. Variation, although extreme, is systematic.

So that we can describe more simply our proposals for computational models that exhibit the same kind of flexibility in our models of vowels, consonants, and transformations of them, we now turn to an overview

TABLE 2.2
Consonant Symbols

	VOICELESS STOP	VOICED STOP	VOICELESS AFFRIC.	VOICED AFFRIC.	VOICELESS FRIC.	VOICED FRIC.	NASAL	GLIDE, LIQUID
BILABIAL	p	b					m	
LABIODENTAL			f	v				
INTERDENTAL			θ (T)	ð (D)				
ALVEOLAR	t	d			s	z	n	l r
ALVEOPALATAL			č (C)	ǰ (J)	š (S)	ž (Z)		
PALATAL								y
VELAR	k	g					ŋ (G)	w
GLOTTAL	ʔ (q)				h			

Words illustrating the consonantal phonetic symbols: p (paw); b (bee); m (me); f (few); v (vie); θ (T) (thaw); ð (D) (the); t (toe); d (doe); s (so); z (zoo); n (no); l (low); r (row); č (C) (chew); ǰ (J) (Joe); š (S) (show); ž (Z) (azure); y (you); k (key); g (go); ŋ (G) (-ing); w (woe); ʔ (ʔ or q) (uh-oh); h (hoe).

of some characteristic sound patterns of American English. We will concentrate on some of the common traits found in many Americans' speech that often pass unnoticed, but which show up well in instrumental analyses of the spoken language.

2.3.1 The act of pronunciation

It is common to speak of pronunciation using terms that connote a generation process. This sort of informal description presupposes a set of relations between a "neutral" or mental representation of a word, dynamic articulatory processes, and patterns of behavior that influence such processes. Such a correspondence between observed phenomena and models is often described in perceptual terms as well. For example, "reduction" or "lenition" can either be thought of either in auditory or articulatory terms—the essence of the process is that a sound is uttered that is perceived as a weak or incomplete version of what it might have been. In phonological practice, it is usual to derive forms from an underlying representation or baseform, a practice that has given rise to the vocabulary of generation.

It is equally possible to reverse the order of description. In contrast, an historical analysis might only make sense in terms of unidirectional, ordered triggering predicates. For morphophonology, reversible machines can be devised such as two-tape finite-state transducers that map between a baseform and a derived form (Koskenniemi 1983a,b;

Karttunen 1983). Any account of the phenomenon is hardwired into the operation of the computer model in either its generation or string acceptance mode. Embedding an account into a model in such a quasi-axiomatic fashion is actually in keeping with the SPE program (Chomsky and Halle 1968). (For reasons that will not concern us here, it should be noted that SPE-style models are not reversible.)

The abstract modeling of variation in pronunciation, with its attendant production/perception ambiguity, can be stated neutrally with respect to generation or recognition, as will become clear in Chapter 5. Yet extremely large dictionaries exist that list baseforms, but that make no claim to listing all possible pronunciations. For certain research, attention therefore must be focussed upon effective methods for generating sets of possible pronunciations from dictionaries. We will return to this topic in the next chapter; now, we will briefly discuss reduction and "strengthening" processes, and the behavior of function words.

2.3.2 Reduction processes

We can group many common pronunciation patterns together under the heading of **reduction** processes. This term signifies that a sound has been "transformed," so to speak, into a more neutral one, a shorter one, or one more like a neighboring sound.

Consider a word such as 'softness'. One can hear that the [t] fuses in a single gesture with the following [n] in this word. (Indeed, the conventional pronunciation now has no [t].) Likewise, if a word such as 'down' follows the final [t] in the word 'soft' in the phrase 'soft down', similar **consonant cluster simplification** ensues. In English, [t] and [d] participate most often in such reduction processes, but other consonants reduce or delete in clusters as well. Part of the challenge in our modeling work has been the specification of the exact environments where consonant cluster simplification occurs.

Consonants also change to other recognizable sounds in such environments. For instance, in the word 'obstacle', the [b] can **devoice** and sound more like a [p] in a process of consonant cluster **voicing assimilation**. In such a case, the vocal folds cease vibrating in anticipation of the upcoming voiceless [s t] cluster. Such change is a change in the **manner** in which a sound is produced. Manner refers to a classification of sound source production, for example, "voiced," roughly meaning, periodic, or "strident," meaning noisy.

The manner of articulation is likewise affected in the process of anticipatory **palatalization**. [t] and [d] may sound more like the affricates [č] and [ǰ] before [r], so that 'tree' and 'droop' sound something like "chree" and "jroop." [y] is associated with this sort of palatalization even between words, as in "betcha" ('bet you').

[y] also influences the articulation of [l] within and across words, as in 'will you' or 'million'. In these cases, the tongue does not reach the position for a full [l] articulation, and instead something like a y-glide is realized.

Assimilations are discussed in terms of **place** of articulation (referring to the vocal tract configuration) as well as manner of articulation. Nasals often assume the point of contact of following stops, as can be heard in "imput" for 'input'. Sometimes the resulting sound is not what is thought of as a regular sound of English, as in the labiodental 'information'. (The palatal nasal in 'onion' is another "non-English" sound.) While many assimilatory changes in American English are anticipatory, some are **perseverative** (this is also called progressive assimilation). Thus, the syllable containing /n/ in 'happen' can be heard as a simple syllabic [m].

The American English speech trait most painstakingly described by researchers involves both place and manner. This is **alveolar flapping**, where non-aspirated alveolar stops ([t, d, n]) become short tongue taps between vocalic phonetic elements. Thus 'butter' can sound as if it has an extremely short [t], or if voicing continues from the vowel through to the syllabic [r], it can sound more like a [d]. This process is an interesting one since a careful specification of the rule's environment involves the role of prosody and word structure.

The other reduction process that researchers most often describe is vowel reduction or deletion, often referred to in general terms as **schwa deletion**. Again, prosodic information forms a part of the description of this phenomenon. Essentially, an unstressed vowel is realized as a short, central phonetic element, or it is deleted. (For example, complete deletion usually is found in the second syllable of 'interesting' in most American dialects.) A more precise characterization of the reduction environment will be found in later chapters, and we will return to the topic in this chapter in the section on function words.

There are many reduction processes in English that occur in syllable-final position. The process that takes /ŋ/ ("ng") to a simple [n] in "somethin" also appears to be related to the stress pattern of the word. Bisyllabic "nothin," for instance, seems more likely to occur in American English than "everythin."

"Dropping g's" is not a new trend in English. Similarly, an ongoing process in many dialects of English is **vocalization of l** in the coda, or consonantal tail of the syllable. [l] can adopt the articulation of the previous tautosyllabic (same syllable) vowel/glide as in 'ball', 'cowl', 'bowl', 'bill' etc. When the vowel is low ('ball', 'cowl'), the change may result in a single, low vowel that exhibits compensatory lengthening signaling the deletion of the [l]. An additional labialized gesture may be seen in other environments replacing [l] in a syllable coda. We can also mention here ways in which an [l] in a coda influences the pronunciation of a preceding vowel. i-detensing describes the substitution of [i] for its lax counterpart [I], as is heard in 'feel' and 'really' ("rilly"). The converse happens as well: lax vowels can tense in this environment in some dialects, so that 'fill' sounds like 'feel' and 'pull' is pronounced with a regular [u].

Another syllable-sensitive dialectal rule is r-deletion. [r] deletes in codas in many dialects on the Eastern Seaboard down around to the Gulf of Mexico (it is not common in Texas). What is popularly known as "intrusive"-r also appears in many of these dialects in intervocalic position, giving rise to "Cuba-r-is" alongside "car is."

2.3.3 Epenthesis and breaking

In contrast to reduction processes, epenthesis and certain processes of vowel "strengthening" make sounds more distinct. "Intrusive"-r, which we just described, is an instance of consonant epenthesis. In a few dialects, r-epenthesis appears after low back vowels in codas containing [š], as in "warsh" for 'wash', and similarly 'squash', and 'Washington'.[3] Epenthesis often is seen in syllable-initial position where there is no onset. 'Drawing', for instance, can obtain a consonant onset with the insertion of an [r] ("draw-r-ing") or a glottal stop. If the first syllable ends with an off-glide, this may become a true onset, as in 'eon' [i yan] or 'go on' [go wan]. In some dialects, an interesting process of "g-insertion" takes place after engma (often parodied with the phrase 'Long G-Island'). Consonant epenthesis in coda position is often more subtle and might be thought of as a side effect of dialect-dependent phonetic timing routines. An often noted phenomenon is the appearance of a [t] in words such as 'prince', making it homophonous with 'prints'.

Epenthetic vowels do occur in English, but not with same regularity as in, for example, Spanish. The most common vowel strengthening process in American English is breaking. Breaking, in which a single vowel splits into two, often accompanies other changes such as vowel raising. Vowel nasalization, too, may accompany these changes in some dialects. On the East Coast, ae-raising/breaking seems to occur most frequently before nasals, but it also appears before fricatives and voiced stops. Linguists have frequently noted its propensity in the high-frequency portion

---

[3]This possibly occurs only in those dialects where there has been a merger of [a] and open-o, but we are not aware of studies along those lines.

of the vocabulary, the function words (such as conjunctions and prepositions, as opposed to content words such as nouns and verbs), so a distinction is heard between 'tin can' (no tensing) and 'I can' (raising of the vowel in the high-frequency auxiliary).

2.4 Function words

Function words include many of the items that serve as syntactic glue in a sentence, such as conjunctions that join individual words or phrases, articles that introduce noun phrases, modals that modulate the meaning of verbs, etc. For any given function word, almost any of its phonetic elements will be reduced or deleted in fluent speech given the appropriate environment. As opposed to content words, function words generally do not have stable regions, such as stressed vowels, which resist deletion in fluent speech. Some peculiarities of function words include:

- vowels can delete in monosyllables
- onsets can delete
- the entire word can delete, leaving a phonological trace in adjacent words

This chapter concludes with examples from the TIMIT database where many of these processes are evident.

Such reduction phenomena are sensitive to context. When function words occur next to one another, the reductions in these strings may become conventionalized. This arises differently in different speaker communities (compare 'it's' and ' 'tis'). A conventional pronunciation makes a sequence of function words phonologically resemble a word (Simpson and Withgott 1986). However, alongside such conventional pronunciations, a range of other possible pronunciations exists, and due to the often stressless nature of these sequences, the deletion and reduction sites do not follow the same patterns as exhibited in content words.

To illustrate, in examining a recorded utterance of 'Gus saw pine trees and redwoods on his walk ...', one is likely to observe that the 'on' is not as prominent as the content words in terms of pitch, energy, or in the duration of the phonetic elements. Also, 'on' is likely to be more prominent than the following word 'his'. Not only can the vowel in 'his' be very short, but the [h] can be deleted entirely. In some dialects, this way of pronouncing 'on his' is virtually indistinguishable from some pronunciations of the single word 'honest' given a weakly articulated final [t] (as in 'he's honest to a fault'). If 'on' is less prominent than 'his', as when the pronoun is emphasized contrastively, the pronoun is more likely to retain the initial [h]. Reduction processes can be responsible for a short schwa plus a nasalized alveolar tap as the pronunciation of 'on'. This specification can be sufficient in order to recognize this lexical item. The vowel in 'on' may be realized as fairly front but it cannot be realized as a true high-front vowel (*[in]). It also seems less likely for the vowel in 'on' to delete as opposed to the vowel in the minimally contrasting phrase 'in his'. That is, 'It's [n] his desk' would probably sound more like 'it's in his desk' than 'it's on his desk.'

Depending on the application, it can be effective to store commonly co-occurring function words together as a single unit in speech processing systems. Some of the most common strings include: 'of the', 'in the', 'to the', 'on the' *etc.* In textual analysis, one finds that hundreds of sequences of function words occur.[4] Another strategy is to develop distinct phone models for function words (Lee *et al.* 1989).

Finally, a linguistic fact about function words that has an impact on pronunciation is the common occurrence of **allomorphy**, or the existence of alternative forms of a morpheme. In English, both 'the' and 'a' have multiple phonetic forms. While the distribution of 'a' versus 'an' is simple to state since it depends on the onset of the following word, 'a' pronounced as schwa instead of as [eʸ], or 'the' pronounced with a schwa versus with an [i], is harder to understand. In the case of 'the', at least there is a correlation of the tensed form with the presence of a vowel-initial word following the determiner. However, 'th[i]' can be observed as a form of emphasis, too. For some speakers, [eʸ] also seems to be an emphasized form. We certainly observe it before consonant-initial words in our database, as in 'touched off a total. . . ', 'hung in a belt', etc. There are also alternate pronunciations of many function words in speakers' idiolects, such as 'didn't' with an epenthetic vowel before the [n].

---

[4]To give an indication of the number of function word strings in English, we list here just some of the ones extracted from the TIMIT data base: and a, and an, and are now, and as, and at the, and because, and can, and even, and even though their, and every, and for which we, and how, and how they, and I, and I'll, and I will, and I've, and in, and is, and is in, and it, and its, and it has, and it may be, and may be, and must be, and not, and of, and on, and one, and only, and/or, and other, and our, and some, and still, and that, and the, and their, and then, and there, and thus, and thus we, and thus are, and to, and to the, and to get a, and want to, and was, and we, and we don't, and we could, and we want to, and what is, and what, and will be, and will then, and with, and which, and would like to, and would, and you, as much as, but with, by our, by the, can be, can do, for a, for each, for the, for you and, for you, from him, I am, I have, in a, in an, in order to, in the, it is it to, not in, of this, of the, on an, on the, so it, that can, the other, this will, to a, to be, to do, to the, you can, we will, will be, will then be, with this and, which will.

2.5 Examples and discussion

To demonstrate the phonological patterns in American English we have described, we now present a number of examples drawn from the TIMIT collection that includes taped speech of informants across the country.

The first four examples illustrate æ-**raising** well, particularly for function words. They also demonstrate that the onset of a function word can delete, as can the entire coda.

(1) 'She   had   your   dark. . .'
    ši   hæ   ǰɹ̩   Affricate from dy
    ši   ε   ǰɹ̩   Deletion of h in function word,
                                                 æ-raising before voiced stop

(2) 'can   be   imagined'
    kεn   bi   æ-raising before nasal
                                                 (function word)

(3) 'only   as   much   money'
    onli   ɪz   mʌč   æ-raising before fricative
                                                 (function word)

(4) 'and   became   lost'
    ɨ   bikem   æ-raising before nasal,
                                                 Cluster deletion [nd]
                                                 (function word)

The next examples also illustrate final consonant deletion, or, as in the case where two identical consonants occur in succession and one deletes, **degemination**. Again, final consonant deletion occurs more regularly in function words.

(5) 'icicles below   our   roof'
             bilo   a   ruf   Degemination of r

(6) 'of   the   command'
    ɨ   ðɨ   Final v deletion before ð

(7) 'that   there   are   no'
    ðɨ   ðεr   ar   no   Final t deletion

(8) 'never   did   make   the'
    nεvɹ̩   dɨ   me   ð   Final d deletion,
                                                 Final k deletion

Initial consonant deletion is rare in content words. Where it does happen, the consonant is usually an [h] or a glide. An example exhibiting initial [h] deletion in a content word is given below in example (12). Consonants in function word onsets delete regularly. Note the deleted [r] in 'through':

(9) 'behind   him'
     biha^ynd ɨm   Initial h deleted

(10) 'is   that   he'
     ɨz   ðɛ   i   Final t deletion,
                                            Initial h deletion

(11) 'through the'
     θ   ðə   r deletion in initial onset,
                                            Final vowel deletion

(12) 'to make their   own   Halloween'
     t me   ðr̩   on   æləwin   Final vowel deletion,
                                            Final k deletion
                                            (content word),
                                            Initial h deletion
                                            (content word)

(13) 'ask   me   to   carry'
     mi   ɨ   Initial t deleted

We could list many more examples of the phenomena we have discussed in this chapter, and add to this list other patterns that characterize American English. Some of these will become apparent in the
discussion of the computer models. Earlier in this chapter, we discussed
the data the models are based on. An interesting property of the data
was the fairly narrow transcription of varieties of schwa. To conclude,
we underscore a few examples of a schwa that has been raised to the
American English sound transcribed as a barred-i. Note that this occurs frequently before [n], and/or after an alveolar sound: 'works as an
impersonal'; 'spurs to the bronc'; 'zippers with a thimble'; '... money,
and must often take'; 'splinter with a pair of tweezers'; 'cigarettes in the
clay'. Also representative: 'humor of the situation'.

Taped and transcribed speech data help to complete the working
environment of the speech researcher. Such data, even supplemented
with machine learning procedures, do not supplant the role of theory
formation in analyzing language. But taken together, a theoretical base
and empirical investigations of such data can prove mutually reinforcing,
or can bring to light weaknesses in either theory, data or technique.
The work described in the following chapters represents one of the first
attempts to bring together theoretical concerns with an analysis of a
large American English database.

3

Predicting possible pronunciations

> *... the program of* SPE[1] *is strikingly similar to that of another fundamental work of twentieth-century thought, Whitehead and Russell's (1910)* Principia Mathematica *... That work enunciated and developed a goal of reducing all of the intellectual content of mathematics to the formal manipulation of expressions in a logistic system by means of fully explicit rules ...*
>
> *We will suggest below that the phonetic arbitrariness which was immediately pointed out as a problem with the* SPE *system ... and that the theory ... which was proposed to remedy this defect, was as inadequate a band-aid for phonology as the theory of types was for the mathematical logic of* PM.
>
> (*Phonology in the Twentieth Century*, Anderson 1985, pp. 329–31.)

One reason it has been difficult to span the gap between a phonological *principia* and the phonetics laboratory has been the relative unavailability of phonetic data for testing phonological hypotheses. The TIMIT and subsequent databases thus offer an opportunity for new types of investigations to take place.

In modeling the phonetic transcriptions in TIMIT, the same fundamental issues that occur in phonological theory are encountered, even though such theory is designed principally to account for sound changes involved in word-formation processes such as affixation. Similar representational concerns emerge, as well as similar issues involving rule ordering. Our experience in modeling a relatively large corpus of phonetic transcriptions using metrically enriched strings has, in fact, led us to the position that rule ordering is largely irrelevant at this level. The other key finding that emerges from our work on modeling pertains to the number of theoretically motivated, seemingly abstract phonological structures that serve as good predictors in the determination of the sound of words in actual recorded speech.

---

[1]SPE is *The Sound Pattern of English* (Chomsky and Halle 1968).

This chapter presents a discussion of context descriptions in rules, and describes an implementation of *machine iteration* of rules and a methodology for statistically analyzing context descriptions in the course of rule development. In Chapter 5, we continue the discussion of techniques for modeling speech using probabilistic rule formulations, still focusing on the use of theoretically-motivated facets of the description, such as sound structure and composition. In this way, we hope to have made headway in crossing between a formalist *principia* and the realm of spoken data.

To develop a computational description of the common pronunciation patterns found in American English, we studied optional rules that employ syllable and foot structure. A set of context descriptors, the rules themselves, and a rule evaluation system were designed and implemented. The context descriptions are based on phonological considerations reviewed in the previous chapters, with special emphasis on findings in the past fifteen years regarding the important descriptive units in the world's languages. While we were familiar with many descriptions of American English rules, and were influenced by prior formulations, we decided to base the rule *mappings* on the TIMIT data. The mappings are the correspondences between phonological transcriptions in the dictionary and phonetically transcribed utterances, leaving aside the context descriptions. As discussed in Chapter 2, these were developed automatically through comparing the TIMIT transcriptions with corresponding pronunciations from an on-line dictionary.

In order to gauge the success of the rules and the mode of ordering, we needed to interpret the rules computationally and apply them to the pronunciations listed as dictionary baseforms. The TIMIT data were used to test coverage, and forms automatically generated by our system were also examined individually. We will describe both the rule interpreter and experimental results in later sections in this chapter and the next, and discuss the final ordering properties of the system. In brief, it was found that rules required no extrinsic ordering, yet categories of rules exist that display distinct ordering behaviors. For instance, some categories of rules are sensitive to information concerning derived/nonderived environments. All rules were applied in all possible orders which resulted in testing a few hundred complex rules at a time. If the issue of rule-ordering is ignored, the resulting system can be viewed as a traditional transformational one, but it is perhaps simpler to think of it as "declarative": there are indeed intermediate representations in an interesting generative sense; however, each intermediate representation also constitutes a valid surface form.

Using metrical and other independently motivated context descriptions to constrain rule overapplication constitutes a more robust methodology than hand-ordering rules in order to block the generation of unlikely pronunciations.

3.1 Rule ordering and postlexical rules

The computational system generates permissible American English pronunciations given a dictionary baseform. The effect of "obligatory rules," such as insuring voicing compatibility between the last element and the plural suffix, are encoded into the dictionary baseform. The operation of the system can be thought of as starting from a "standard" transcription listed in a computer file, then computing variants that one is likely to observe when given transcribed speech.

In Chapter 1, issues concerning phonological rule ordering were reviewed. Most work on this topic has focused on morphology and related *lexical* phonological phenomena. In contrast, rules that operate when words are organized together for conversation, the *postlexical* component of the phonological grammar (Kiparsky 1981; Mohanan 1982), are less well-studied in terms of their ordering behavior. These rules comprise not just the rules that apply to sounds at word boundaries, but also the rules that describe "casual pronunciation." We model optional, postlexical rules that describe such pronunciation.

The application of the lexical rules of English is characteristically *obligatory* (Kiparsky 1981; Mohanan 1982). This means that if a rule fails to apply, the form will be aberrant. In contrast, a large class of postlexical rules apply *optionally*. Rules that always apply—either low-level rules or lexical rules—are often those whose environment specifies word-internal information.[2] For instance, true English stop aspiration, an obligatory rule, is sensitive to word-internal information such as whether or not the lexical item is a function word. It applies word-initially in content words regardless of how the previous word ends—even if the phonetic element is an [s], a context usually fatal to stop releases. Such obligatory rules are like lexical rules, too, in that their misapplication or omission affects grammaticality judgments, or at least judgments of native ability. Not aspirating stops in certain environments is as foreign sounding as saying, for example, "profoundity" for 'profundity' with its lax vowel. Aspiration stands in contrast to the optional rule of flapping in that not flapping a [t]

---

[2]Often but not always: alongside such low-level, obligatory rules that observe word boundaries, some obligatory rules have been noted that apply across-the-board (without regard to word-boundary information), such as rules of epenthesis that break apart vowel sequences.

in certain speech settings may sound somewhat unusual, but still appears to be a stylistic choice rather than sounding like a non-native speaker.

The same issues that make the general problem of rule ordering hard resurface for optional, postlexical rules. These issues revolve around rule interaction, representational issues such as the abstractness of the symbol string, and what information is encoded in the string apart from segmental information. We did not model the morphological structure of a word. However, the importance of morphological structure in the analysis of low-level pronunciation has been noted in the past (*e.g.*, Withgott 1982). In that analysis, it is argued that aspiration, but not flapping, is sensitive to morphological structure. For instance, the input form for 'militaristic' is 'military', where the [t] is characteristically released, as opposed to the [t] in 'capitalistic', where it is likely to be tapped or flapped (and compare 'capital' where the [t] need *not* be released). A released [t] is argued to block flapping. Thus it is only necessary to look for unreleased [t]'s in the right segmental environment as candidates for flapping, such as the one in 'capitalistic/capital'.

This analysis is consistent with the behavior of the generation system which models optional rules such as flapping with no access to morphology.[3] It would be of theoretical interest to locate counterexamples to this mode of generation for American English, that is, pronunciations produced by low-level optional rules which must have access to labeled morphological bracketing as opposed to, for instance, metrical structure and segmental information.

3.2 More on rules: interactions, representations and formal language theory

In discussing rules, we describe operations over sets of strings of symbols. String manipulation has been extensively explored in terms of its formal behavior (in the context of natural language, see Barton *et al.* 1987). Venneman, Hooper, and several other linguists in the 1970's advocated that phonological representations should be, in essence, forms similar to those that occur naturally in speech. This was a controversial move away from the formalist tradition of the 1960's. The newer representations were described as less *abstract*.

In order to penetrate the issues surrounding abstractness of represen-

---

[3]Caveat: While the system does not compute morphological structure, it does have access to coarse category information, namely the function word/content word distinction.

tation, rule ordering and optional rule application, consider an example consisting of just two strings: language L contains the lexical entries ABCDE and ABFDE. After rule application, lexical items appear as *abfge* and *abfde*. Assuming a set of identity rules (A → a), there appear to be at least two kinds of rule ordering solutions in formulating a successful derivation.

Derivation 3.2.a: non-occurring intermediate forms

forms	ABCDE	ABFDE
D → G after C	"ABCGE"	–
C → F before G	ABFGE	–
output	abfge	abfde

Remember that the sequence *abcge* never occurs in L. Here the proscribed form is used as a bridge over to the actually occurring string. This type of solution is at the heart of the "abstractness" controversy just alluded to. It inserts special symbols into the strings in order to trigger the right output, and then these special symbols are deleted. The reason such a solution strikes many as unrevealing is its unconstrained nature: any string can be generated, not only those that occur in natural language.

A variant of the special symbol solution is to permit intermediate *strings* in the derivation which never occur in the language, rather than non-occurring symbols.

Suppose one wanted to avoid dummy symbols and non-occurring strings. A strategy that uses neither is to annotate the symbol string with additional types of information. (See Kiparsky's 1968 discussion on the use of diacritics.) An instance of this was seen in the example of Sea Dayak nasalization, where we hazarded the guess that syllable structure played a role in the derivation (see Section 1.1).

Along with metrical structure, another type of information that can be carried along in the derivation is whether the symbols have been rewritten, or if they constitute the baseform. Peet notes that acoustic differences exist between the same allophones with different derivational histories (Peet 1988). In a study of American English palatals, these differences prove significant when comparing both duration and preceding vowel formant values. For instance, comparing examples such as 'toss sheepskins' and 'josh Sheila', Peet finds that the [š] derived from a sequence of two [š]'s exhibits longer duration values than the [š] from an [sš] sequence, reflecting the original phonetic element duration values. We will use the prime symbol (′) to mark a symbol that has been derived.

Derivation 3.2.b: derived environments

forms	ABCDE	ABFDE
C → F before D	ABF'DE	–
D → G after F'	ABF'GE	(doesn't apply—F is not derived)
output	abfge	abfde

This solution has the merit that the derivation can stop at any point and the resulting string is contained in the string set of L. Whether or not *abfde* occurs as a version of ABCDE would be a point to determine, were this a real language. If it did occur, this sort of strategy would seem to be viable. This example derivation has served to highlight the issues that arise in designing a system for the optional postlexical rules in an actual language. To summarize, some questions that occur are: Can dummy symbols or non-occurring, "intermediate" forms be avoided? Is there a difference in the application of rules to derived and to non-derived dictionary symbols? We can also ask: does the use of secondary structure such as syllable position appear to be motivated?

3.2.1 Formal language theory

One article on rule ordering from the perspective of formal language theory is of particular relevance because it demonstrates the equivalence and strength relations of competing rule ordering schemes (Pelletier 1980). Pelletier wishes to convince the reader that sufficient constraints should be placed on a linguistic theory so as to limit the possible *languages* that it can describe. This is in contrast to merely placing restrictions on the kinds of *grammars* (rule systems) used (see Wasow 1978 for a discussion). In effect, Pelletier argues that strong beliefs about rule ordering merely reflect restrictions on the grammar and are not related to constraining the linguistic description. Writing large rule application programs is a good way to appreciate Pelletier's point of view. The moral we draw from our rule generation system is that rule environments and memory-efficient algorithms count for more than rule ordering schemes.

Kaplan and Kay have discussed how a cascaded rule system can be compiled down to an unordered phonological generator or acceptor because, in general, phonological rewrite rules define regular relations (Kaplan and Kay 1981). That is, rules in a grammar that have a *Total Ordering* in Pelletier's terminology can be recast into a composite operation. The compactness in our formulation, however, is achieved primarily through multiple applications of the same rule component. The sort of compilation Kaplan and Kay discuss is difficult to achieve because rules apply in all possible orders. (This sounds similar to what

Pelletier terms a *Quasi Ordering* but is different because each rule is *optional*.) In general, compiling a finite-state machine[4] to encode a large rule system displaying all possible orders would result in a very large machine. However, if the application of rules is optional, all possible orders will be observed if the output of a machine representing any arbitrary order is fed back into the same machine, and the process is continued until no new forms are observed. The condition that no new forms are observed is crucial in placing a bound on the computation. This form of "checklist" is equivalent to keeping track of paths already explored in a graph search. Additionally, the rules that insert a symbol are bounded by either the number of applications permitted or by the checklist mechanism. The computer model is finite-state because the size of the graph is bounded by the size of the interactions of the rule set in the Pronunciation Prediction System (PPS) (which is merely large, the derivation is not arbitrarily long) despite the appearance of rules notated in a context-free format, as we will now see.

The rule system described in the next section could be implemented as a *two-level* system in which the relation of baseforms to phonetically transcribed output forms is constrained by two-tape finite-state transducers. (See Koskenniemi 1983a,b); Karttunen 1983.) That is, a machine might be constructed that directly maps between a lexical entry and a possible pronunciation, in either direction. (For instance, we encoded 102,000 pronunciations into a determinized and minimized finite state network containing 5,000 states and 16,000 transitions.[5]) However, we focused on constructing a probabilistic finite-state mechanism (as discussed in Chapter 5). There are practical problems in constructing an analogous two-level probabilistic system if the entire context of the top and bottom levels are to be considered.

One interesting property of the system described in this chapter is the ability to "jump off" at any point in the derivation in the mapping between dictionary entries and possible pronunciations—that is, to halt the computation at any output stage and return a valid string. This property is not discussed in any of the standard formal language sources we are familiar with.

---

[4]Finite state machines play a central role in computational linguistics and natural language processing. An FSM can be thought of as a highly restricted embodiment of an automaton that processes a string of symbols and, in a finite amount of time, accepts or rejects the string as directed by a program. At the other end of the restrictiveness spectrum are the automata known as Turing Machines. See Hopcroft and Ullman 1969.

[5]We constructed this network with Ron Kaplan. The numbers cited in the text reflect straightforward, unoptimized determinization and minimization.

3.3 Developing context descriptions and rule statements

In this section we describe the context descriptions used in order to prevent rule overapplication, and we list two hundred or so rules to give a sense of the computational system. It is not necessary to read through each rule—they are provided primarily as a matter of interest to the phonologist or rule developer. We then turn to issues regarding rule ordering.

In Chapter 2, we described the distinct behavior of function words. One context descriptor, therefore, is whether or not the intended site of the rule application, the *target*, lies within a function word. Two other simple context descriptors describe the presence of immediately adjacent phonetic elements, as is shown in Table 3.1.

The phonological symbols are referred to as "characters" in the formulation; they are not implemented as distinctive features because the overhead involved in both developing the rules and writing the interpreter for distinctive features is too great. Let us emphasize that using unitary characters rather than distinctive features was a purely implementational convenience in this model.

One reason why distinctive features would have been preferable is that their use reins in the descriptive power of symbol-to-symbol mappings. For instance, in this implementation, it is as simple to state 'a → p' as 'a → ʌ'. The fact is lost that one rule is exotic (it would involve changing all the component features of the sound) and the other commonplace (it would involve a simple feature substitution). To convert this system to a distinctive feature specification is not a simple matter of replacing single characters with distinctive-feature strings, or it shouldn't be, for alternative characters in the contextual environment are permitted such as:

("r"   NIL   (:function-word (:following "θ" "f")))   ; *"through, from"*
old   new   context description   examples

This says that [r] is deleted after the voiceless fricatives [θ] or [f] in function words. While it is not difficult to establish the intersection of the features to pick out these (and only these) phonetic elements, it creates extra work for the system's interpreter in actually applying the rules. In fact, in the probabilistic models (Chapter 5), as opposed to the rules here, each environment is split apart and similar environments are algorithmically combined, so it doesn't matter if distinctive features or a single symbol short-hand is employed.

Here are some rule examples as implemented in the lisp system. The first symbol, x, is a dictionary symbol that is rewritten as y when the

TABLE 3.1
Simple Context Descriptors

Context Descriptor	Test
:function-word	Is the target in a function word?
:preceding [char-list]	Is the target just before one of the characters in [char-list]?
:following [char-list]	Is the target just after one of the characters in [char-list]?

contextual description is met. The contextual predicates are interpreted conjunctively except when in a list after a modifier such as ":following", in which case an "or" is implicit between the listed symbols after the modifier:

("x"   "y"   (:descriptor (:element-location "a" OR "b")))   ; *"word"*
old   new   context description   examples

Notice that some of the rules in Table 3.2 apply anywhere in a function word; others are subject to an additional segmental constraint by the ":preceding" and ":following" context descriptors.

The complement of a character set can also form a context descriptor. In the following rules, note the use of ":not-preceding." This sort of restriction is not much discussed in phonological theory. The problem often displayed by this kind of context description are attempts to falsify it: One is never sure if enough data have been collected for a rigorous test. Below, note too the rule that rewrites a [ur] as a simple syllabic r. Because non-occurring intermediate forms are proscribed, this has been stated as a single rule instead of a sequence of rules. Table 3.3, then, specifies a few rules for function words constrained *not* to apply before certain phonetic elements.

Word-initial and -final position are often referred to in traditional descriptive phonological work. Indeed, both environments prove useful in describing postlexical rules. These are listed in Table 3.4.

Particularly in the case of function words, where phonetic element changes are found abundantly in the data, word-boundary phenomena appear only to apply at boundaries, and not "across-the-board." For instance, some consonant voicing and devoicing processes seem to apply at word edges regardless of the structure of the surrounding words, yet behave in a context-sensitive fashion within words. Table 3.5 provides a partial list of word-boundary phenomena. The first half uses the function word context descriptor; the second describes general word-boundary rules.

TABLE 3.2
Rules Specifying Function Word Contexts

("h" NIL	(:function-word))		; "his"
("d" NIL	(:function-word (:following vowel "n")))		; "should, did, and, around"
("u" "ɪ"	(:function-word (:following "t")))		; "to, you"
("u" "i"	(:function-word (:following "t")))		; "to"
("u" "ɨ"	(:function-word (:following "y" "t" "d")))		; "to, do, you"
("u" "ə"	(:function-word))		; "to"
("u" "ʊ"	(:function-word))		; "to, you"
("ʊ" "ə"	(:function-word))		; "would"
("u" NIL	(:function-word (:following consonant)))		; "to, do, you"
("a" "ʌ"	(:function-word))		; "what, are, not"
("ɛ" "ə"	(:function-word (:preceding "m")))		; "them"
("æ" "ə"	(:function-word))		; "an, and, at"
("æ" "ɛ"	(:function-word))		; "than, has, there, and, ;had, an, that, at, can"
("o" "ə"	(:function-word))		; "so, almost"
("ʌ" "ɨ"	(:function-word (:preceding "z")))		; "does"
("ʌ" "ɪ"	(:function-word (:preceding "z")))		; "does"
("ʌ" "ɛ"	(:function-word (:preceding "s")))		; "just"
("i" "ʉ"	(:function-word (:following "š")))		; "she"
("o" "ʉ"	(:function-word (:following "f")))		; "for"
("ɪ" "ɛ"	(:function-word))		; "him"
("ɪ" "ʊ"	(:function-word (:preceding "l")))		; "will"
("ɪ" "ə"	(:function-word))		; "with, his"
("ɪ" "ɨ"	(:function-word))		; "is, in, this, it's, without"
("ɛ" "ə"	(:function-word (:following "w" "aʷ") (:preceding consonant)))		; "whenever"
("ð" "θ"	(:function-word))		; "this, the, that"
("aʷ" "a"	(:function-word (:preceding "r")))		; "our, ourselves"

Along with word boundary context descriptors, a dozen or so context descriptors record the metrical structure of a word. These are listed in Table 3.6.

In order to make use of these context descriptors, a syllable and foot parser was written to identify and mark the corresponding boundaries in an on-line dictionary. The pronunciation is notated as a string of characters drawn from a phonetic alphabet. The phonetic structure contains a list of syllables, which are structured into feet. Every phonetic character in the phonetic string is contained in exactly one syllable, and each syllable is contained in exactly one foot. A dictionary is a collection

TABLE 3.3
Rules Specifying Function Word Contexts And Negative Environments

("ɔ" "ə" (:function-word (:not-preceding "ə")))	; "on"
("ɹ" "ɹ̩" (:function-word (:following "aʷ" "ɪ") (:not-preceding "ɹ")))	; "near, our"
(("ʊ" "ɹ") "ɹ̩" ((:following "y") (:not-preceding "ɹ")))	; "purists, your, cured, uremia"

of phonetic structures, keyed by their orthographic transcription. An extract from the dictionary looks like this:

```
sanctum s@Gk1-txm
sand s@nd1
sandbank s@nd1*/b@Gk2
```

Mappings to the transcription string yield, for example, two dictionary symbols that map to a single phonetic element, as shown in Figure 3.1 below.

The parts of the syllable (onset, nucleus, coda) are represented procedurally, as will be described below. Table 3.7 lists a partial set of rules that specify foot and syllable information.

The other sort of metrical information of interest is the specification of stress, as shown in Table 3.8. Each syllable in the dictionary has a stress mark (0=unstressed, 1=primary stress, 2=secondary stress). Syllables that are newly created through the processes of vowel epenthesis and resyllabification are assigned 0 stress, as will be discussed below. Rules containing context descriptions that refer to stress are among the most numerous, as can be seen in Table 3.9.

The rules presented in this section provide a representative sample of the context descriptions and rules contained in the PPS. There is another class of context descriptions and rules not yet described that pertain to rule ordering. Before that description, it will be helpful to explain the operation of the rule interpreter.

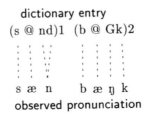

dictionary entry
(s @ nd)1 (b @ Gk)2

s æ n   b æ ŋ k
observed pronunciation

FIGURE 3.1 Transduction between a dictionary entry and one observed pronunciation. The word is "sandbank."

TABLE 3.4
Descriptor: Position in Word

CONTEXT DESCRIPTOR	TEST
:word-initial	Is it the first phonetic element in the word?
:word-final	Is it the last phonetic element in the word?

TABLE 3.5
Position in Word

("t" "d"	(:function-word :word-initial))	; "to"
("v" NIL	(:word-final :function-word (:following vowel)))	; "of, have"
("a" "ə"	(:word-initial :function-word))	; "are"
("f" NIL	(:word-final :function-word (:following vowel)))	; "off"
("z" NIL	(:word-final :function-word (:following vowel)))	; "these"
("æ" "ʌ"	(:function-word :word-initial))	; "as"
("æ" "ɪ"	(:function-word :word-initial))	; "as, an, and, at"
("o" "ɪ"	(:function-word :word-final))	; "for"
("θ" NIL	(:function-word :word-final))	; "with"
("š" "č"	(:word-initial :function-word))	; "should"
("č" "š"	(:word-initial :function-word))	; "you"
("y" "č"	(:word-initial :function-word))	; "you"
("ð" NIL	(:function-word :word-initial (:preceding vowel)))	; "the, that"
("ə" "l̥"	(:word-initial :word-final :function-word))	; "the" (before word-initial "l")
("aʷ" "ʌ"	(:word-final :function-word))	; "how"
("w" NIL	(:word-initial (:function-word (:preceding vowel))))	; "was"
("u" "r̥"	(:function-word (:word-final)))	; "to"
(NIL "q"	(:word-initial (:preceding "r̥")))	; "earn"
("i" "ɪ"	(:word-final))	; "me, oily"
("t" "ɾ"	(:word-final (:following "l" vowel)))	; "felt, at, put, ate, suit, what, it, but, not, about, set"
("t" "d"	(:word-final (:following consonant)))	; "looked, touched, locked, attacked"
("n" "n̩"	(:word-initial))	
("m" "m̩"	(:word-initial))	; "muscular"

TABLE 3.6

Metrical Structure

CONTEXT DESCRIPTOR	TEST
:foot-initial	Is the target the first phonetic element in some foot?
:foot-final	Is the target the last phonetic element in some foot?
:syllable-initial	Is the target the first phonetic element in some syllable?
:syllable-final	Is the target the last phonetic element in some syllable?
:first-syllable	Is the target the first syllable in some word?
:last-syllable	Is the target the last syllable in some word?
:open-syllable	Is the target in a syllable that has no coda?
:syllable-containing [phonetic element]	Is the target in a syllable containing the given phonetic element?
:onset	Is the target part of the onset of a syllable?
:onset-cluster	Is the target part of the onset cluster ($>$ 1 consonant) of a syllable?
:coda	Is the target part of the coda of a syllable?
:coda-cluster	Is the target part of the coda cluster ($>$ 1 consonant) of a syllable?
:tautosyllabic	Is the whole left side of the rule within a single syllable?

3.4   Rule interpreter

The rule interpreter processes the context descriptions and rule statements just described. It was implemented by Steven C. Bagley. While some of the symbol replacement mechanism was straightforward to implement, insuring that the context descriptors behaved correctly was sometimes difficult, and the rule ordering algorithms involved much experimentation, as will be described below.

In the implementation, a *phonetic structure* is a data structure describing a particular pronunciation of a word. The pronunciation is either a dictionary entry, or the result of applying a rule to a previously existing pronunciation. A rule can contain any number of non-conflicting context descriptors.

The execution of a rule takes the phonetic structure that matches the rule's left-side and context, and creates a new phonetic structure, a copy of the original, and performs the indicated modifications to its structure. *Replacement* changes the old characters to the new characters, starting from the target position, and leaves the target at the beginning of the replacement. *Deletion* removes one or more characters and leaves the target at the position of the deletion.

Insertion inserts new characters starting at the target position, and leaves the target at the left of the insertion (so its position with respect to the left end of the word does not change). When inserting between syllables, new characters are added to the beginning of the syllable to the right, unless at the end of the word, in which case the characters

TABLE 3.7
Feet and Syllables in Rules

("t" "glottal" (:foot-final (:following vowel "n" "l")))	; *"joint, right, point, print,*
	;*promote, outpost, yoghurt, adult"*
("ǰ" "ž" (:foot-initial))	; *"juice"*
(NIL "glottal" :foot-initial (:following vowel) (:preceding true-vowel)))	
;true-vowel excludes e.g., syllabic "ṇ"	; *"my(q)opia"*
("ŋ" "n" (:foot-final (:preceding "g")))	; *"mango"*
("t" "glottal" (:syllable-final (:preceding consonant)))	; *"gently, shorten,*
	;*appointment"*
("ə" "l̩" (:syllable-final (:preceding "l")))	; *"avalanche"*
("n" "ŋ" (:syllable-final (:preceding "g")))	; *"ingredients"*
("ə" NIL (:open-syllable :unstressed :word-initial))	; *"approval"*
("ə" "r̩" (:unstressed (:following "r") (:preceding consonant) :first-syllable))	
	; *"remote"*, not *"irregulaRIty"*
(("r" "ə") "r̩"(:tautosyllabic :last-syllable (:preceding consonant)	
(:not-preceding "r̩")))	; *"children"*
("z" "s" (:syllable-final :coda))	; *"prefers"*
("a" "ɨ" (:function-word :last-syllable))	; *"are"*
("æ" "ɨ" (:function-word :last-syllable))	; *"at, can, and, there's, have,*
	;*an, that, has"*
("o" "ɨ" (:function-word :last-syllable (:preceding consonant)))	; *"for"*
("ʌ" "ə" (:function-word :last-syllable))	; *"one, from, but"*
(("ʌ" "m") "m̩" (:function-word :last-syllable))	; *"from"*
("ɪ" NIL (:function-word :last-syllable (:preceding "n")))	; *"in"*
("ɔ" "ɨ" (:function-word :last-syllable))	; *"on"*
("ə" "ɛ" (:word-initial :open-syllable))	; *"attention"*

TABLE 3.8
Stress

Context Descriptor	Test
:unstressed	Is the stress of the syllable = 0?
:stressed	Is the stress of the syllable = 1?
:secondary-stress	Is the stress of the syllable = 2?

are added to the end of the previous syllable, *e.g.*, (notating a syllable boundary with "—"):

> Insert new vowel after old vowel
> before: $V_1C_1—C_2V_2C_3—C_4V_3$
> insert: V_i after V_2
> gives: $V_1C_1—C_2V_2—V_iC_3—C_4V_3$

> Insert new vowel before old vowel
> before: $V_1C_1—C_2V_2C_3—C_4V_3$
> insert: V_i before V_3
> gives: $V_1C_1—C_2V_2C_3—C_4V_i—V_3$

Whenever the execution of a rule creates a new syllable, that syllable receives a stress of 0 since epenthetic vowels are not normally stressed in English. Recall that the subparts of the syllable are represented procedurally. This choice was made because of the dynamic nature of the derivation—syllable boundaries do not remain fixed. The *vowel* (nucleus) of the syllable is defined as the first simple vowel in the syllable, or the first vowel, if there are no simple vowels. A vowel is simple if it is not also a consonant. The *onset* of a syllable contains all those characters before the vowel. The *coda* of a syllable contains all those characters after the vowel. The onset or coda is a *cluster* if it has more than one character in it.

3.4.1 The Prediction Pronunciation System and its ordering properties

To review the reasons why hand-ordering rules is not as attractive an option as allowing context descriptions to limit generation, one can list: (a) the difficulty of determining correct order; (b) the difficulty of debugging large, ordered rule sets; and (c) the temptation rule-ordering carries with it to use dummy symbols and/or intermediate non-occurring bridging strings in the derivation. Finally, we can't claim definitively why the most focused rule ordering work has been associated with the use of strings without secondary structure (such as syllable structure), but we think it is because the one can serve to displace the other, as argued for the example Sea Dayak problem (Section 1.2.4). To the extent that such secondary structure plays an explanatory role in language description, its omission is a deficiency.

The PPS limited generation by the use of context descriptions, operating as follows: A dictionary baseform was evaluated and a new form was produced after every successful rule application. Onsets, nuclei and codas are computed anew as the metrical structure of a word changes in the course of the derivation. Therefore, this information is not contained

TABLE 3.9
Stress as a Context Description

(("y" "u") "ɨ" (:tautosyllabic :unstressed (:following consonant)))   *"contributed"*

(("ɨ" "n") "ṇ" (:unstressed (:not-following "y" "s" "z")))   ; *"intelligence, broken
;interpretation"*

(("ɨ" "n") "ṇ" (:unstressed (:preceding consonant) (:not-following "y")))
      ; *"sufficiency, emergency, perpendicular, original, occasionally"*

("ə" NIL (:unstressed (:following "r") (:preceding "n")))   ; *"foreign"*

("ə" "ṛ" (:unstressed :word-initial (:preceding "r")))   ; *"arrange, around"*

(("ɔ" "r") "ṛ" (:tautosyllabic :unstressed (:not-preceding "ṛ")
      (:following "p" "t" "k" "f")))   ; *"forbidden"*

("ɪ" "ə" (:original-nucleus :unstressed (:preceding consonant)
      (:not-preceding "ŋ" "y")))   ; *"exclusive, evaluate, coexist, emerge, cement"*

("i" "ə" (:unstressed (:following "d") (:not-preceding "ŋ" "y")))
      ; *"development, regarding"*

("i" "ə" (:unstressed (:preceding "r")))   ; *"before"*

(("o" "r") "ṛ" (:unstressed (:not-preceding "ṛ")))   ; *"original"*

(("ɛ" "r") "ṛ" (:stressed (:not-preceding "ṛ")))   ; *"sheriff, heroism, their, very"*

(("ɛ" "r") "ṛ" (:secondary-stress (:not-preceding "ṛ")))   ; *"military"*

("ə" ("y" "ɨ") (:unstressed (:following "i")))   ; *"ingredients"*

(NIL "č" (:secondary-stress (:following "t") (:preceding "u")))   ; *"costumes"*

("ʌ" "ə" (:secondary-stress))   ; *"luxurious"*

("ʌ" "ə" (:unstressed))

("ʊ" "ə" (:unstressed))   ; *"superbly, could"*

("u" NIL (:unstressed (:preceding "l" "l")))   ; *"spectacular, casual, actually"*

("u" "ɨ" (:secondary-stress (:following "y")))   ; *"stimulating"*

("a" "ə" (:unstressed))   ; *"Vietnamese"*

("ɛ" "ɨ" (:unstressed (:preceding "n")))   ; *"when"*

("ɛ" "ə" (:unstressed))   ; *"when, them"*

("æ" "ṛ" (:stressed (:preceding "r")))   ; *"carry"*

("æ" "ɨ" (:unstressed (:preceding "n" "d" "t")))   ; *"advance"*

("o" "ə" (:unstressed))   ; *"Hallowe'en, heroism"*

("ɪ" "ɨ" (:unstressed (:original-nucleus)))   ; *"clothing, intelligent, voyage,
;atypical, silhouette"*

("i" "ɨ" (:unstressed))   ; *"review"*

("ɪ" "ɨ" (:secondary-stress (:original-nucleus)))   ; *"shellfish"*

("ṛ" "r" (:unstressed (:preceding vowel)))   ; *"several, history"*

("ḷ" ("ə" "l") (:unstressed (:not-preceding "l")))   ; *"violence, marvelously,
;people"*

("ṇ" "n" (:unstressed (:preceding vowel)))   ; *"glistening"*

("ɔ" "a" (:original-nucleus :stressed (:preceding consonant)))   ; *"wash, on,
;pathological"*

("ž" "z" (:original-onset :unstressed (:following vowel) (:preceding vowel)))
      ; *"exposure"*

("t" "ɾ" (:onset :unstressed (:following vowel "r") (:preceding vowel)))
      ; *"computer, quality, bottom, better, eating, Autumn, inferiority, competing,
;getting, exotic, idiotic, Saturday, citizen, curiosity, meeting, exacerbated,
;autographs, haughty, exhibited, thirty, forty, dirty, artists, parties"*

TABLE 3.10
Derived Status

Context Descriptor	Test
:original-onset	Is the target part of the onset of a syllable, and has that onset not been modified in any way from the original dictionary entry? (That is, is it not a derived onset?)
:original-nucleus	Is the target the nucleus of a syllable, and has that nucleus not been modified in any way from the original dictionary entry?
:original-coda	Is the target part of the coda of a syllable, and has that coda not been modified in any way from the original dictionary entry?
:once-only	Is this rule being applied to this word for the first time?

in the dictionary baseforms. The rules were unordered and each rule was tried once. This constituted one *rule application generation*. Then, each newly derived form was resubmitted to the rule set until a new generation was completed, and so forth. A serial lisp processor was used for this implementation, but each generation of rule application could have been performed in parallel. This mode of application will be termed *machine iteration*. We experimented both with stopping rule generation at arbitrary generation counts and letting the process terminate when no new forms had been created. Such a process of rule application is not possible to try with pencil and paper using hundreds of rules. It is, as can be imagined, computationally expensive in terms of memory. (The runtime on a small scientific workstation (a Symbolics 3650) was several days for dictionaries of just under twenty thousand items.)

In addition to the context descriptors listed above, four context descriptors were developed which addressed the need to distinguish dictionary baseforms from derived results. Let us emphasize that a derived result is not a non-occurring, "bridge" form—it counts as a generated pronunciation, as do forms further generated from it. The four context descriptors are shown in Table 3.10.

The basic function of the *:once-only* context descriptor was to prevent epenthesis rules from infinitely inserting phonetic elements. Such reapplication represents a simple loop in a finite-state machine, and would probably be best prevented outside the rule system. For instance, *mirage* is often pronounced, not with a schwa, but with a syllabic r in the first syllable which is reinforced, as it were, with a true [r] as the

TABLE 3.11
Once-Only Rules

(NIL "ə" (:stressed :once-only (:following "e") (:preceding "l")))	; *"male"*
(NIL "ə" (:function-word :once-only (:following "ɪ") (:preceding "m")))	; *"him"*
(NIL "r" (:once-only (:following "ṛ")))	; *"authorized, mirage"*
("ε" "ɪ" (:once-only (:following consonant) (:preceding "n" "ŋ" "m" "r" "k" "t")	
(:not-following "l")))	; *"ephemeral, experiments, getting, object,*
	;*academic, many, then"* (not in *"vocabulary"*)

following onset. [r]'s in just this position can be syllabified through an independent process. But this shouldn't lead to a string of syllabic r's of the form [mṛṛṛ ... ṛraž], even if it is possible to say! The other use of the *:once-only* context descriptor appeared when a complement to a mapping existed; this prevented the derivation from endlessly flipping back and forth between two forms. Some example rules that use this predicate are illustrated in Table 3.11.

The remaining context descriptors are of more interest. They distinguish a dictionary baseform symbol from, for example, one that is inserted through epenthesis. For instance, sometimes a vocalic phonetic element can be added to a consonant-initial word. This merely sounds as if the speaker is preparing to talk; however, spectrally, the sound can be classified as an [ɪ]. Yet this front "vowel" will not tense in the same way the vowel in *enough* will. Distinguishing such cases looks well-motivated. Table 3.12 lists rules with the non-derived ":original-x" predicate.

3.4.2 Experimental results

There are three standard ways to evaluate rule systems. One is to make rule statements available to a community of knowledgeable critics. Second, rules can be embedded in a synthesis or recognition system and performance can be analyzed. A third way is to test for coverage against a database.

We examined samples of rule output from the PPS ourselves, and asked a linguistics graduate student to independently examine the samples. This is in attempt to check for cases of *overgeneration*. A methodology for statistically evaluating the context descriptions for a given rule or for a given dictionary symbol was then developed. These methods check both overgeneration and descriptive adequacy. Coverage was also tested by generating forms and observing words found in the TIMIT data not generated by the rule system *coverage*. The topic of coverage will be discussed in the next chapter.

The output of the rules was compiled into automata that are efficient

TABLE 3.12
Non-Derived Environments

("ɪ" "i" (:word-initial :original-nucleus :open-syllable))	; *"emergency, enough"*
("ɨ" NIL (:open-syllable :original-nucleus (:following "r" "r̩") (:preceding consonant)))	
("ə" NIL (:open-syllable :original-nucleus (:following "r" "r̩") (:preceding consonant)))	
("r̩" "ə" (:original-nucleus :unstressed (:preceding consonant)))	; *"survive,* *;government"*
("ɪ" "ə" (:original-nucleus :unstressed (:preceding consonant) (:not-preceding "ŋ" "y")))	; *"exclusive, evaluate, coexist,* *;emerge, cement"*
("ɪ" "ɨ" (:unstressed (:original-nucleus)))	; *"clothing, intelligent, voyage,* *;atypical, silhouette"*
("ɪ" "ɨ" (:secondary-stress (:original-nucleus)))	; *"shellfish"*
("ɔ" "a" (:original-nucleus :stressed (:preceding consonant)))	; *"wash, on,* *;pathological"*
("e" "ɪ" (:function-word :original-nucleus))	; *"they, always"*
("ɛ" "ɪ" (:function-word :original-nucleus))	; *"many, then"*
("ə" "ʌ" (:function-word :original-nucleus))	; *"a, of"*
("ə" "ʌ" (:word-initial :original-nucleus))	; *"aluminum"*
("ə" "ʌ" (:last-syllable :original-nucleus :unstressed))	; *"Sheila, amoebas,* *;vodka"*
("d" "glottal" ((:preceding "n̩") (:original-nucleus)))	; *"students"*
("ɪ" "i" (:original-nucleus (:preceding "r̩" "R" "ŋ")))	; *"year, think"*
("ə" "ɨ" (:original-nucleus (:following "θ" "t" "d" "r" "s")))	; *"lithographs,* *;superb, unbeatable"*
("ə" "ɨ" (:original-nucleus (:preceding "m" "n" "ŋ", "v" "z" "s" "š" "č" "j", "b" "d" "t" "p", "i") (:not-following "g")))	; *"Nevada, divorced"*
("ɨ" "ɪ" (:original-nucleus (:not-following "ɾ") (:not-preceding "d")))	; *"nonprofit"*

finite state acceptors over strings. These are recognition networks without probabilities. A method for carefully adding probabilities to finite state networks based on appropriate contextual factors is the central topic of Chapter 5. First, however, we return to context descriptions and their interactions.

3.5 Context interactions in predicting pronunciations

Appropriate contextual descriptors can aid in predicting the probability of a phonological variant. In what we will refer to as the "log-linear" experiments, log-linear modeling was examined as a method for finding sets of contextual descriptions which are correlated with the observed pronunciation of a dictionary baseform.

3.5.1 Log-linear modeling

In modeling phonological variation, a set of contextual descriptors, or *factors*, such as preceding context and stress, characterize the context in which a dictionary symbol is observed as a particular phone. If each factor can take on one of several *categorical* values, then the factors can be represented as separate dimensions in a *multi-dimensional contingency table*. An example of a two-dimensional contingency table is shown in Figure 3.2. (This table is for illustrative purposes only.)

| | | PHONETIC ELEMENT | | | |
		s	š	z	–
	primary	157	24	10	31
STRESS	*secondary*	20	3	2	5
	unstressed	296	104	49	53

FIGURE 3.2 Illustrative Contingency Table

The two factors in this table are **phonetic element** and **stress**. The phonetic element factor has the four categorical values [s], [š], [z], and **deleted**. The stress factor has the three categorical values shown in the table. Each *cell* in the table contains a count of the number of tokens having the set of values represented by the cell. Each set of values is composed of one value from each factor. For example, the upper left cell in Figure 3.2 represents the observation that in a total of 157 tokens in the data, the value of the factor **phonetic element** was [s] and simultaneously, the value of the factor **stress** was **primary**.

Log-linear modeling is a statistical technique useful for analyzing the relationships between factors in a multi-dimensional contingency table. The distribution of counts in the cells of a contingency table is modeled as a combination of independent factors and *interaction terms*, which capture the relationships among factors that are not independent. Log-linear modeling enables one to find a model which adequately describes the observed data with a minimal level of interaction terms. The log-linear modeling methodologies used in this study are based primarily on those described in Fienberg 1985 and Bishop, Fienberg, and Holland 1977. As in Fienberg's work, only sets of hierarchical models were examined. For such models, inclusion of higher-order interaction terms requires inclusion of the related lower-order interaction terms. By comparing two models differing only in one interaction term, one can determine whether or not the extra term contributes significantly to the simpler model. This method was used to assess the *main effect* of each of the contextual factors on the predicted phonetic elements.

3.5.2 Pronunciation data

The dictionary baseforms were compared with the phonetic transcriptions of the "sx" sentences in TIAP's 4 through 20 of the DARPA TIMIT database. In particular, each dictionary symbol was *mapped* to the corresponding phonetic element in the phonetic transcription. In the case of deletion, the dictionary symbol was mapped to *nil*. Log-linear modeling was used to analyze the effect of different lexical contextual factors on the mappings. The computed mappings and the associated lexical context of each mapping were entered into a database. The lexical contexts examined in this study are described by a set of contextual factors which include:

1. preceding dictionary symbol,
2. following dictionary symbol,
3. stress of the syllable the dictionary symbol is in (primary, secondary or unstressed),
4. syllable part (onset, nucleus, or coda), and
5. whether or not the dictionary symbol is at a word boundary (*i.e.*, word-initial only, word-final only, not at a word boundary, both word-initial and word-final).

A separate model was created for each dictionary symbol since there was no reason to assume that different dictionary symbols have similar models. The mappings from a dictionary symbol to an phonetic element (a substitution) or nil (a deletion) are modeled together for each dictionary symbol because the contexts of the mappings are identical. In contrast, insertions were modeled separately from substitutions and deletions since they occur *between* dictionary symbols. For example, given the phonemic sequence /ans/, the /n/ may be deleted, substituted, or it may match its canonical form. But in the case of insertion, pairs of dictionary symbols are examined for an epenthetic phonetic element between them. For example, the sequence pair /ns/ may be examined for an inserted [t].

Statistics characterizing the number of sentences and words in the corpus are shown in Table 3.13. All studies were performed on the entire corpus. Based on empirical observation, several authors (see Fienberg 1985) have noted that reasonable estimates may be obtained with a minimal expected cell count of only one sample per cell for large contingency tables. In this work, tables which did not contain an adequate number of tokens were not analyzed.

TABLE 3.13
Statistics of the sx TIAP's 4-20

Number of Sentences	974
Number of Word Tokens	7340
Number of Word Types	1791

Although most of the combinations of contexts and dictionary symbols had an adequate number of tokens in the database, a few combinations did not. This is due to the variable number of tokens in the database per dictionary symbol, as expected, as well as to the variable number of observed categories in a contextual factor per dictionary symbol. For example, /s/ can be deleted or realized as one of three phonetic elements ([z], [s], [š]) but /t/ can be deleted or realized as one of ten phonetic elements ([θ], [pʰ], [dʳ] (release only, no closure), [tʳ], [D], [ɾ], [dʰ], [tʰ], [dʳ], and [ɾ̃]). Thus, given the same number of /s/ and /t/ tokens, and all the other dimensions being identical, the expected number of tokens per cell for /s/ would be almost three times as large as that expected for /t/. As another example, the number of applicable values for the contextual factor **syllable part** is not the same for all dictionary symbols. For instance, /t/ may appear in either the onset or coda, but /h/ only appears in the onset.

Table 3.14 displays the distribution of insertions, deletions, matches, and substitutions and the total number of samples in the data we examined. Overall, except for the alveolar plosives and /ž/, which has a small sample size, plosives and fricatives were mapped to their canonical form over 90% of the time. Vowels and syllabics exhibited a large number of substitutions. The syllabic substitutions appear to be due to labeling many of the syllabics as [vowel] [semivowel]. The large number of vowel substitutions may be due in part to vowels being perceived as a continuous phenomenon. In contrast, consonants are thought to be perceived more categorically. Consequently, we singled out consonants for analysis.

3.5.3 Results

Log-linear models for each of the consonants were evaluated and several phonological rules were examined. In particular, a model which does not contain a term modeling the interaction between the *mapping factor* and any *contextual factor* was compared to a model with an interaction term between the mapping factor and one contextual factor. Because the lexical context was known, an interaction term composed of all contextual factors examined was included in both models. This term accounts for all interactive effects among the contextual factors,

TABLE 3.14

Distribution of Mapping Types in a Subset of TIMIT

	DELETION (%)	INSERTION (%)	MATCH (%)	SUBSTITUTION (%)	N
u	0.5	0.0	78.7	20.8	602
ᴜ	28.3	1.9	44.3	25.5	212
o^y	0.0	0.0	95.2	4.8	105
o	9.9	0.0	67.2	22.8	583
i	0.7	0.4	91.3	7.6	1080
ɨ	17.1	5.9	51.9	25.1	526
ɪ	4.8	0.2	51.5	43.5	1401
e	0.0	0.2	97.6	2.2	503
ɛ	2.9	0.6	85.8	10.8	695
a^y	0.2	0.4	97.3	2.2	511
ə	6.3	3.5	38.3	51.9	1876
a^w	0.0	0.0	90.0	10.0	201
ɔ	2.2	0.0	84.0	13.8	500
ʌ	5.5	0.7	83.4	10.4	451
æ	1.9	0.0	68.0	30.1	834
a	5.7	0.0	88.0	6.3	583
r̩	0.4	2.2	84.1	13.3	271
n̩	0.0	1.3	52.6	46.2	78
m̩	0.0	0.0	5.9	94.1	17
l̩	1.3	0.0	83.4	15.3	235
unstressed r̩	1.2	0.5	61.0	37.2	562
m	0.3	0.0	96.7	3.0	901
n	1.0	0.3	90.3	8.3	1717
ŋ	0.3	0.0	92.0	7.7	299
r	3.3	1.2	75.3	20.2	1634
l	2.5	0.2	93.6	3.7	1226
w	1.4	4.0	94.6	0.0	575
y	16.5	6.2	72.6	4.7	340
h	14.1	2.3	83.5	0.0	389
p	0.1	0.0	99.3	0.5	764
t	7.4	1.7	84.2	6.7	1869
k	0.4	0.1	99.1	0.3	1150
b	0.6	0.0	99.2	0.2	660
d	11.5	1.0	85.9	1.6	1188
g	0.7	1.7	96.9	0.7	414
č	0.4	0.4	96.3	2.9	243
ǰ	0.7	0.0	96.0	3.4	297
s	0.9	0.0	97.1	2.0	1498
š	0.0	1.4	98.3	0.3	291
z	0.2	0.0	93.6	6.3	1072
ž	0.0	4.5	61.4	34.1	44
f	1.0	0.2	98.8	0.0	576
θ	2.2	0.0	90.7	7.0	227
v	0.8	0.0	96.9	2.3	481
ð	0.8	0.6	96.1	2.4	622

TABLE 3.15
First Set of Contextual Factors and Best Models

	PRECEDING MANNER	FOLLOWING MANNER	SYLLABLE PART	BEST MODELS
l	0.001	0.001	0.001	(prec manner & next manner) & (syll position)
r	0.001	0.001	0.001	prec manner & next manner & syll position
m	>.05	>.05	0.05	independent
n	0.001	0.001	0.001	(next manner & syll position) & (prec manner & syll position) OR (prec manner & syll position) & (prec manner & next manner)
ð	0.001	>.05	>.05	prec manner
š	>.05	>.05	>.05	independent
f	0.001	0.001	0.001	next manner
s	0.001	0.001	0.001	prec manner & next manner & syll position
v	>.05	0.005	0.05	next manner
z	>.05	0.001	0.005	(prec manner & next manner) & (syll position)
b	0.001	0.001	0.001	syll position & prec manner next manner & prec manner
d	0.001	0.001	0.001	(next manner & syll position) & (prec manner & next manner) (prec manner & syll position) & (prec manner& next manner)
k	0.001	0.001	0.001	prec manner & next manner & syll position
p	0.001	0.001	0.001	prec manner & next manner & syll position
t	0.001	0.001	0.001	(prec manner & syll position) & (prec manner & next manner)

independent of the phonological to phonetic mappings. Thus, the effect of an additional interaction term in predicting phonetic behavior was assessed independently of the interaction of contexts among themselves.

Because of the large number of combinations of preceding and following dictionary symbols, several classifications based on distinctive features for characterizing the preceding and following underlying context were attempted. A description based on six manner of articulation classes, fricative, plosive, nasal, vowel, liquid-or-glide, and none (if sentence-initial or sentence-final), was found to produce models in which the classes interacted with the mappings, indicating that the representation encompasses useful information. In contrast, a description with five classes based only on place of articulation, front, mid, back, other (for diphthongs, liquids and glides), and none (if sentence-initial or sentence-final), was not found to be informative for most dictionary symbols. Therefore, in models with the contextual factors of preceding dictionary symbol and/or following dictionary symbol, a class description based on manner was used to represent those contexts.

Contextual Factor Set 1

For each of the dictionary symbols in Table 3.15, the significance level of the main effect of each of three contexts—preceding manner class, following manner class, and syllable position—upon dictionary symbol mappings is shown in the second through fourth columns. The significance was quantized to six levels: less than or equal to .001, greater than .05 and between the following values with equality allowed on the upper bound, .005, .01, .025, and .05.

The "best model" for describing the data observed with each dictionary symbol is shown in the last column of Table 3.15. Each model is composed of one or more interaction terms separated by an ampersand, with grouping indicated by parentheses. For example, in the best model for /l/, preceding manner class and following manner class jointly and syllable position independently influence the realization of /l/. The "best model" is defined here to be the model(s) with a minimal level of interacting terms and for which the null hypothesis (that the model correctly fits the data at the 0.05 significance level) cannot be rejected.

Each of the three contextual factors exhibits significant interaction with the plosive mappings; furthermore, several of the plosives required higher order interaction terms to provide an adequate model of the mappings, given that the contexts are known. Models in which information would be lost if a dimension is collapsed (*i.e.*, a contextual factor, such as preceding manner is ignored) include those for /t/ and /d/. The contexts of following manner class and syllable position did not appear to have significant interaction on mapping for the dictionary symbols /ð/ and /š/. As expected, when a single context is adequate to explain the resulting mapping, one of the most significant terms is obviously in the model (*e.g.*, preceding manner for the /ð/ model).

Contextual Factor Set 2

The significance level of the main effect on dictionary symbol mappings of the contexts word boundary, stress, and syllable part is shown in Table 3.16. None of the contextual factors for the dictionary symbols /ð/, /š/, and /θ/ exhibit a significant interaction with the dictionary symbol mappings, indicating that this set of contexts is not useful in predicting these mappings. This fact is reflected in the best models, which indicate the independence of the mapping factors and the contextual factors, as

Table 3.16

Second Set of Contextual Factors and Best Models

	Word Boundary	Stress	Syllable Part	Best Models
l	0.001	0.025	0.001	word bdry & stress & syll position
r	0.001	> .05	0.001	(stress & syll position) & (word bdry & syll position) OR (stress & syll position) & (word bdry & stress)
m	0.001	0.001	0.001	(word bdry & stress) & (stress & syll position)
n	0.001	0.001	0.001	(word bdry & stress) & (stress & syll position)
ð	> .05	> .05	> .05	independent
š	> .05	> .05	> .05	independent
θ	> .05	> .05	> .05	independent
f	0.001	0.001	0.001	word bdry & syll position
s	0.001	0.001	0.001	stress & word bdry
v	0.025	> .05	0.025	(word bdry & syll position) & (stress)
z	> .05	0.005	> .05	independent
č	0.001	0.025	0.01	word bdry
ǰ	0.001	0.001	0.001	word bdry & stress & syll position
b	0.001	> .05	0.001	(word bdry & syll position) & (word bdry & stress) OR (stress & syll position) & (word bdry & stress)
d	0.001	0.001	0.001	(word bdry & syll position) & (stress & syll position) OR (word bdry & syll position) & (word bdry & stress)
g	0.001	0.001	0.001	(stress & syll position) & (word bdry & syll position) OR (stress & syll position) & (word bdry & stress) OR (word bdry & syll position) & (word bdry & stress)
k	0.001	0.01	0.001	(stress & syll position) & (word bdry & syll position) OR (stress & syll position) & (word bdry & stress) OR (word bdry & syll position) & (word bdry & stress)
p	0.001	0.001	0.001	(stress & syll position) & (word bdry & syll position) OR (stress & syll position) & (word bdry & stress) OR (word bdry & syll position) & (word bdry & stress)
t	0.001	0.001	0.001	(stress & syll position) & (word bdry & stress)

shown in the third section of the last column of Table 3.16. The lower half of the last column of the table shows that once again, interaction terms are required to model many of the plosives.

This study indicates that some contextual factors can have significant interactions. If a subset of contextual factors must be chosen, as when building a recognition system, the subset with significant interactions should not be ignored. Otherwise, some information will not be utilized and the resulting model will be less good. A simple example illustrating this point is shown in Figure 3.3.

| | | TEMPERATURE | |
		warm	freezing
PRECIPI-	yes	no	yes
TATION	no	yes	no

FIGURE 3.3 Weekend in the Mountains?

The table may be used by someone who likes to go to the mountains only if they can ski in the snow or swim in a mountain lake. In the table, the decision on whether to spend the weekend in the mountains is dependent on the interaction of the factors temperature and precipitation; a warm temperature by itself does not increase the probability of going to the mountains. Thus, a decision based on temperature and precipitation independently is not as good as one in which the interaction of both factor values is considered simultaneously. Similarly, when higher order interactions between the contextual and mapping factors are present for a dictionary symbol, a better model results if the interactions are included in the model.

3.5.4 Detailed examples

We now examine three well-known phonological phenomena to illustrate a method for investigating the role of different context descriptors. The phenomena are *glottalization, final plosive deletion, and schwa deletion.* First, the commonly-held belief that glottalization is sensitive to the specification of stress in vowel-initial words was examined. Since the relative contribution of several variables, including the preceding environment, was compared, sentence-initial vowels were not used in the study. Explanatory factors were stress, the manner of the preceding dictionary symbol and the manner of the following dictionary symbol. The response factor was the presence or absence of glottalization. Table 3.17 shows the significance level of the main effect of each contextual factor and also shows the best model for predicting the presence of

TABLE 3.17
Glottalization Preceding Word-Initial Vowels

	Stress	Preceding Manner	Following Manner	Best Model
Significance Level	.001	.001	> .05	stress & prec manner

TABLE 3.18
Word-Final Plosive Deletion

	Stress	Preceding Manner	Following Manner	Best Models
t	.001	.001	.001	stress & prec manner & next manner
d	.001	.001	.025	(stress & prec manner) & (prec manner & next manner)

glottalization. The main effects indicate that the factor **stress** does have an important effect on glottalization, but so does the **preceding manner** class. The model indicates that the combination of stress and the manner of the preceding dictionary are needed to model the data well. In contrast, the dictionary symbol following the vowel (**following manner**) is not important. This example illustrates that neither contextual factor alone provides an adequate model.

Next, the contexts in which final alveolar plosive deletion occurs was investigated. The contexts used were manner of the preceding dictionary symbol, manner of the following dictionary symbol, and stress. Although initially all plosives were considered, /b/ was excluded due to lack of sufficient data to produce reasonable estimates. No examples of word final deletion of /g/, /k/, or /p/ were observed in the database and so they were excluded also. The remaining plosives, /d/ and /t/, were examined separately; the results are displayed in Table 3.18. In both cases, stress and manner of the preceding and following dictionary symbols play an important role in determining whether or not a deletion occurs.

The following dictionary symbol also proves to be important in /t/ deletions. In the simplest adequate model of /d/ deletion, stress and the preceding manner interact to affect deletion, and the preceding and following manner of the dictionary symbol also interact to affect deletion. In the best model of /t/ deletion, each context separately and independently affects the mapping. Thus the results suggest that /t/ and /d/ deletion should be modeled independently.[6]

---

[6]The following are words from the TIMIT corpus in which a "t" was observed to be deleted (deleted "t"'s are indicated by ()'s): ac(t)s, Almos(t), Ambidex(t)rous,

Whether or not the preceding manner class, following manner class, and stress were important to schwa deletion was also investigated. The results indicate that each context as a main effect is important, but that an adequate model requires interaction among all three contexts.

This methodology is useful in several ways. The computed models provide information as to whether or not contextual factors separately influence mappings, and whether or not higher order interactions exist among the contextual factors. When higher order interactions do exist, context dimensions must be collapsed carefully, if at all. If it is known that a chosen set of contexts strongly influences phonological to phonetic mappings, the probability of a particular phonetic realization given a set of context values can be estimated (from either the model estimates, the actual counts, or some other estimates, such as pseudo-Bayes). The probabilities, in turn, can be combined to provide an estimate of a given phonetic realization of a word. By examining the results in detail and testing specific linguistic hypotheses, as we described for word-initial glottalization and word-final plosive deletion, a better understanding of phonologically-induced variability can be developed.

3.6 Conclusions

The context description set used by production rules in computer systems usually lack any reference to either metrical structure or to the derived status of a dictionary baseform. In such systems, overgeneration is restricted by means of rule-ordering. In contrast, an enriched context description set was investigated for our PPS and found to be adequate as a trade-off for relaxing rule order.

Several hundred mappings that account for variant pronunciations of words in common American English dialects were developed, along with the PPS program which applies all rules in all possible orders until no new forms are produced. Each rule includes a set of one or more context descriptors. Some of the interactions between descriptors was explored

---

An(t)arctic, appoin(t)ed, artis(t)s, atheis(t)s, a(tt)acked, bes(t), Biologis(t)s, blis(t)ered, cas(t), ca(t)'s, coas(t), collec(t)s, consis(t)s, Con(t)inen(t)al, couldn'(t), coun(t)ed, coun(t)y, crisscrosse(d), depic(t)s, developmen(t), didn'(t), discoun(t), divorce(d), documen(t)s, Don'(t), effec(t)s, en(t)er, en(t)ertaining, exhibi(t)ed, fores(t), Gen(t)ly, ge(t)s, gif(t)s, gigan(t)ic, governmen(t), haun(t)ed, iden(t)ical, ins(t)rumen(t)s, in(t)erview, I(t)'s, jus(t), kep(t), lates(t), main(t)enance, mee(t), Mosqui(t)oes, mos(t), motoris(t)s, mus(t), neares(t), neglec(t), no(t), Objec(t)s, oin(t)men(t), orien(t)al, overlooke(d), paren(t)al, paren(t)hood, paymen(t)s, permanen(t), plan(t)ed, precinc(t)s, presen(t)ed, preven(t)ed, processe(d), produc(t)s, projec(t), purchase(d), puris(t)s, reflec(t), reflec(t)s, relaxe(d), repain(t)ed, repain(t)ing, serpen(t)'s, shocke(d), splin(t)er, s(t)rong, subjec(t), tas(t)es, tha(t), (t)o, unin(t)errupted, vege(t)ables, was(t)e, Westches(t)er, zoologis(t).

through log-linear modeling, and the interactions of the descriptions and rules as a whole was explored by generation and inspection. We now examine the coverage exhibited by the PPS, and turn to a question raised by the similarity between resulting forms engendered by a large system.

4

Word confusion, sound stability

One of their kings, called Samalvāhana, i.e., in the classical language
Śātavāhana, was one day in a pond playing with his wives, when he said to
one of them Māudakaṃ dehi, i.e., do not sprinkle the water on me. The
woman, however, understood it as if he had said modakaṃ dehi, i.e., bring
sweetmeats. So she went away and brought him sweetmeats. And when
the king disapproved of her doing so, she gave him an angry reply, and
used coarse language towards him. Now he was deeply offended, and in
consequence, as is their custom, he abstained from all food, and concealed
himself in some corner until he was called on by a sage, who consoled him,
promising him that he would teach people grammar and the inflexions of
the language. Thereupon the sage went off to Mahādeva, praying and fast-
ing devoutly. Mahādeva appeared to him, and communicated to him some
few rules, the like of which Abul'aswad Addu'alī has given for the Arabic
language...This was the beginning of the science of grammar. (from 'An
Accurate Description of All Categories of Hindu Thought,' Abū Raihān
al-Bīrūnī 1030.)

The fact that words are articulated in various ways, and the fact
that they are heard in unintended ways, are unchanging properties of
language. What is ultimately understood depends on what sort of pronunciation processes exist (which is a specifiable part of language) and
what the lexicon contains (also a specifiable part of language). Thus it
should be possible to predict, in gross terms, what sort of recognition
errors people make, and with some understanding of the front end, the
sort of errors machines make. All else being equal, it should also be possible to know what parts of a sound sequence should be given the most
weight in determining the identity of a word. This chapter investigates
such inter-word *confusability* and sound *stability* in a discussion of the
lexicon's sound structure.

One tool for examining stability and confusability is a computational
system for producing alternate pronunciations of a word. Such a system

was the Pronunciation Prediction System (PPS) described in Chapter 3. We found that three forms of context descriptions are useful in limiting the generation of pronunciations not observed in the transcribed sentences (the issue of *overgeneration*) and that the enriched set of context descriptors was adequate for generating the pronunciations observed in the data without the use of hand-determined rule-ordering (the issue of *coverage*).

4.1 Lexical competition in large vocabulary recognition

The PPS can be used to investigate word similarity because it provides an algorithmic means for identifying similar sound strings which originate from dissimilar sources. Word similarity is of course an issue of interest for speech recognition system builders. It is a given that vocabulary size and permitted syntactic complexity influence the performance of a speech recognizer, and that in word-spotting tasks, fewer false positives are returned if the target word is in some sense phonologically unusual. These three factors—vocabulary size, the space of phrasal contexts for words and the degree of word similarity—have all been studied and reported on to some extent in the psychological literature on word access by human subjects. Such perceptual studies demonstrate that word similarity and word frequency effects govern human performance. These observed psycholinguistic effects are suggestive for the design of ambitious recognition systems.

Most models of human lexical access, like speech recognizers, emphasize some form of competition among similar words. One of the best known psychological models of candidate selection in word access is the *cohort theory* (Marslen-Wilson and Welsh 1978). According to this theory, a cohort, which contains words that exhibit acoustic-phonetic similarity, remains active until enough information is gleaned for the listener to select a unique lexical member as the recognized word. This theory followed upon work by Landauer and Streeter which demonstrated relationships between word frequency and word similarity neighborhoods (in essence, cohorts) (Landauer and Streeter 1973).

A wordlist can be restructured in *n*-dimensions so that the distance between items reflects the degree of similarity between them. For such a similarity space, Landauer and Streeter observed that the most dense regions contain the most frequent words. (Note that this is not an automatic property of word frequency—high-frequency words could be phonologically dissimilar.) Such psycholinguistic work recalls Zipf's interest in modeling sound change as a function of sound "conspicuousness," for which he developed a similarity scale. His law, which notes the zeta distributions of word types according to the frequency rank of their types (Zipf 1935), has been modified many times in order to better model lexical distributions, and continues to be a starting point for analyzing similarity relations in the lexicon (*e.g.*, Baayen 1991). For unrestricted speech recognition tasks, where dialects may vary widely and syntactic information may be of limited utility, it is important to calibrate the extent of the problem of word similarity given the best possible front-end.

How does a system select among potential *confusors* within a cohort? (For the moment, let us define a confusor of word w as a distinct word x which becomes homonymous with w when either w or x is casually pronounced.) For instance, weighting schemes could be developed which take word frequency into account, or the recency of having encountered the candidate word could be modeled (Scarborough, Cortese, and Scarborough 1977, and see the discussion of the dynamic cache at the end of this chapter). Alternatively, it may be advisable to attempt to extract the gist of a passage without determining a (unique) best string of lexical items (Chen and Withgott 1992).

Luce reports on psychological and computational studies designed to refine the notion of a *similarity neighborhood* as he develops a perceptual theory of lexical access which he terms the *Neighborhood Activation Model* (Luce 1986). Luce uses two methods to compute neighborhood density in his experiments. One is to obtain a Hamming distance[1] by simple substitution, deletion, or insertion of a given sound in any position in a transcription, as is common practice in word similarity modeling. For instance, Luce lists /p@t/, /kIt/, /k@n/, /sk@t/, and /@t/ as neighbors of 'cat' /k@t/ (p. 15). Surprisingly, this admittedly phonologically naive scheme succeeds as a weak indicator of how hard it is to access a word—words in high density neighborhoods were recognized with less accuracy by subjects in a word recognition experiment. For this experiment a large subset of the 20,000 entry Merriam Webster Pocket Dictionary was used. In a more sophisticated experiment, 800 CVC monosyllables were tried. The substitutions in this experiment were drawn from perceptually-based phoneme confusion matrices. The confusion probabilities preserve consonant position (word initial and final position) but leave aside other contextual factors such as neighboring sound. This more modest, but phonologically more realistic experiment

---

[1]A Hamming distance is simply the number of bits which differ between two vectors. Cf. Viterbi and Omura 1979, p. 81: "Suppose that the received vector $\mathbf{y} = (y_1, \ldots, y_n)$ differs from a transmitted vector $\mathbf{x}_m = (x_{m1}, \ldots, x_{mN})$ in exactly d_m positions. The number d_m is then said to be the *Hamming distance* between vectors x_m and y … "

lends stronger support to the hypothesis that neighborhood density plays an important role in word recognition.

We might think of Hamming distance augmented with confusion matrix data as a measure of, roughly, abstract phonemic similarity. Although sound confusion data is perceptual is origin, the environments in which substitutions are made must also be taken into account in order to model the sort of phonetic phenomena observed in actual speech.

4.1.1   Using rules to investigate similarity neighborhoods

As we have seen in Chapter 3, American English speech contains pronunciation patterns markedly different from those that can be modeled by indiscriminate single segment changes or changes based on CVC confusion matrices. For instance, the rules presented in the previous chapter model patterns of variation including changes in the syllable structure of a word. Accepting Luce's conclusion that neighborhood density is a significant factor in recognition, and observing that the PPS produced large sets of variant forms from the word lists, as was described in the last chapter, we could ask: How severe is the problem of inter-word confusability in a realistically large space of possible pronunciations? How severe is the problem if word boundaries are not known? What natural constraints are helpful in disambiguating potential confusions? What properties of vocabularies makes them potentially confusable?

4.1.2   Coverage experiments

In order to say something reasonable about word neighborhoods, we needed to establish a measure of the *coverage* of the generated word variants over the corpus. We used five lexicons in the coverage experiments:

1. A subset of the TIMIT database consisting of the 1800 words used in the phonetically balanced sentences labeled "sx."
2. A subset of the Brown corpus consisting of the 1800 most frequent words cited
3. A subset of the Brown corpus consisting of the 2800 (actually, 2798) most frequent words
4. A word list was constructed from 2000 low-frequency words that do not appear in the Brown corpus.
5. A corpus consisting of 20,000 words including many of the words in the other lists.

The lexicons contain phonetic transcriptions with syllable, foot, and stress information indicated. The experiments using the PPS were performed in collaboration with Steven C. Bagley.

The TIMIT data were used to test coverage, and generated forms were also examined individually. The PPS was configured as described in the previous chapter. This produced many variant forms. As an example, Table 4.1 shows the output of all seven generations of the item *crocodile*.[2]

For this word, sixty variant forms were generated before no new pronunciations appeared. We are tempted to believe that the earliest generations produce the most common forms, but testing this idea would have required a balanced distribution of speakers across dialect groups to produce these words. It is evident that the PPS undergenerates, if all (even monolingual) American speech communities are carefully considered. For example, monophthongization of [aʸ] (substituting the diphthong with a simple vowel such as [aː]) is not represented. This is because the mappings were derived from a particular set of data where many dialects are not represented.

We are able to determine easily whether or not we miss actually occurring pronunciations in the TIMIT data. We tested 4291 lexical items. The 4291 word *types* were the result of several speakers reading 500 sentences. As described in Chapter 2, the sentences contain a variable number of words. The system found 213 unpredicted variant words, which meant that the PPS correctly generated 99.95% of the pronunciation *tokens*. The forms that were produced by the readers but not generated by the system are listed in the appendix. Based on this result, we felt that gross coverage of the dialect-dependent and individually varying pronunciations represented in the TIMIT data was not a problem. In summary, we demonstrated that it is possible to achieve good coverage of the TIMIT database by trading extrinsic ordering restrictions on the PPS in favor of enriched context descriptions.

Moreover, by examining forms generated from several wordlists, we obtained a gross measure of where the rules most often applied; we will turn to the question of what parts of a word are the most stable below. Stability is of great interest in determining the similarity of works in actual speech. We also compared the number of identical variants produced from different dictionary baseforms for these wordlists to get a measure of inherent confusability, as we will now describe.

4.2 Confusability

We performed a series of experiments investigating sets of confusable words. Words are said to be confusable when a single observed pronunciation derives from more than one dictionary baseform. Homonyms

---

[2]The symbol ə̥ here indicates a devoiced schwa.

TABLE 4.1

BASEFORM **crocodile** [(kral-kə) (da^{y}l2)]

Generation 1:	[kra] [kɨ] [da^{y}l]	[kra] [kə̥] [da^{y}l]
	[kra] [kə] [ɾa^{y}l]	[kra] [kə] [da^y] [l̩]
Generation 2:	[kra] [kɨ] [da^y] [l̩]	[kra] [kə̥] [da^y] [l̩]
	[kra] [kə] [ɾa^y] [l̩]	[kra] [kə] [da^y] [yl̩]
	[kra] [kɨ] [ɾa^{y}l]	[kra] [kə̥] [ɾa^{y}l]
	[krak] [da^{y}l]	[kra] [kɪ] [da^{y}l]
Generation 3:	[kra] [kɪ] [ɾa^{y}l]	[kra] [kɪ] [da^y] [l̩]
	[krak] [ɾa^{y}l]	[krak] [da^y] [l̩]
	[kra] [kɨ] [da^y] [yl̩]	[kra] [kə̥] [da^y] [yl̩]
	[kra] [kə] [ɾa^y] [yl]	[kra] [kə] [da^y] [yəl]
	[kra] [kə] [da^y] [yɨl]	[kra] [kə] [da^y] [yɪl]
	[kra] [kə] [da^y] [yʌl]	[kra] [kɨ] [ɾa^y] [l̩]
	[kra] [kə̥] [ɾa^y] [l̩]	
Generation 4:	[kra] [kɨ] [da^y] [yʌl]	[kra] [kə̥] [da^y] [yʌl]
	[kra] [kə] [ɾa^y] [yʌl]	[kra] [kɨ] [da^y] [yɪl]
	[kra] [kə] [da^y] [yɪl]	[kra] [kə] [ɾa^y] [yɪl]
	[kra] [kə] [da^y] [yɪ] [l̩]	[kra] [kɨ] [da^y] [yɨl]
	[kra] [kə] [da^y] [yɨl]	[kra] [kə] [ɾa^y] [yɨl]
	[kra] [kɨ] [da^y] [yəl]	[kra] [kə] [da^y] [yəl]
	[kra] [kə] [ɾa^y] [yəl]	[kra] [kɨ] [ɾa^y] [yl̩]
	[kra] [kə] [ɾa^y] [yl]	[krak] [ɾa^y] [l̩]
	[kra] [kɪ] [ɾa^y] [l̩]	[krak] [da^y] [yl]
	[kra] [kɪ] [da^y] [yl]	
Generation 5:	[krak] [ɾa^y] [yl]	[krak] [da^y] [yəl]
	[krak] [da^y] [yɨl]	[krak] [da^y] [yɪl]
	[krak] [da^y] [yʌl]	[kra] [kɪ] [ɾa^y] [yl]
	[kra] [kɪ] [da^y] [yəl]	[kra] [kɪ] [da^y] [yɨl]
	[kra] [kɪ] [da^y] [yɪl]	[kra] [kɪ] [da^y] [yʌl]
	[kra] [kɨ] [da^y] [yɪ] [l̩]	[kra] [kə̥] [da^y] [yɪ] [l̩]
	[kra] [kə] [ɾa^y] [yɪ] [l̩]	[kra] [kɨ] [ɾa^y] [yəl]
	[kra] [kə] [ɾa^y] [yəl]	[kra] [kɨ] [ɾa^y] [yɨl]
	[kra] [kə] [ɾa^y] [yɨl]	[kra] [kɨ] [ɾa^y] [yɪl]
	[kra] [kə] [ɾa^y] [yɪl]	[kra] [kɨ] [ɾa^y] [yʌl]
	[kra] [kə] [ɾa^y] [yʌl]	
Generation 6:	[kra] [kɨ] [ɾa^y] [yɪ] [l̩]	[kra] [kə] [ɾa^y] [yɪ] [l̩]
	[krak] [ɾa^y] [yʌl]	[kra] [kɪ] [ɾa^y] [yʌl]
	[krak] [ɾa^y] [yɪl]	[kra] [kɪ] [ɾa^y] [yɪl]
	[krak] [ɾa^y] [yɨl]	[kra] [kɪ] [ɾa^y] [yɨl]
	[krak] [ɾa^y] [yəl]	[kra] [kɪ] [ɾa^y] [yəl]
	[krak] [da^y] [yɪl]	[kra] [kɪ] [da^y] [yɪl]
Generation 7:	[krak] [ɾa^y] [yɪl]	[kra] [kɪ] [ɾa^y] [yɪl]

are inherently confusable. Words such as 'ladder' and 'latter', 'and' and 'an', or 'an' and 'in' which share at least one pronunciation, or variant, are also confusable. This definition of confusability is markedly different from a Hamming distance between word pairs where output strings are compared and the number of symbol differences calculated. In information theoretic terms, such a metric employed to compare output strings conflates the properties of the source, the channel, and the decoding process where the source is the pronunciation process, the channel is the acoustic transmission of the sound, and the decoding is the interpretation by a listener. Luce, by using data from confusion matrices, was able to remove certain effects of the decoding process. In these studies we model certain properties of the source.[3] Using the TIMIT 1800-corpus, we found that 192 pronunciations were phonologically confusable with at least one other word.

Words in a common cohort were then disassociated if they had no syntactic category feature in common. Thus 'fairy' and 'very' disassociate, but 'few' and 'view' do not, since both have the feature N. The features serve as a rough indication of similarity of usage in speech; for instance, the N-marked items 'few' and 'view' can both serve as subjects. We employed nine category based features: CONJ, ADV, PRO, COMP, PREP, DET, ADJ, N, V. Such a gross set of features serves to break apart some confusability cohorts, but it leaves others untouched. For example, we classified nouns inflected with a possessive marker ('s) simply as N, even though the distribution of such suffixed nouns and other nouns is somewhat different. The same thing can be said for count *versus* mass nouns, singular *versus* plural, and so forth.

Such category based features had some effect on breaking apart confusability cohorts. When such syntactic information was considered, the number of confusable words decreased to 132 from 192. The average number of words confused with a given word was 3.76 words; this number falls to 1.83 when syntactic category information is added. The maximum number of confusions fell from 18 to 9; the median remained at 1.

4.2.1 Monosyllabic word confusions

The uncommon-2000 lexicon, which contains only low frequency words, and thus more content words, proved to have the *fewest* confusions. This lexicon also had the *greatest* number of variants produced by far. Thus the number of variants does not directly mirror the amount of confusability. One likely account of the observation would involve the

---

[3]Channel effects might also be modeled. See, *e.g.*, Bell, Dirks and Carterette 1989.

TABLE 4.2
What Words Are Confusable With Others?

Length Characteristics	sx-1800	Brown-1800	Uncommon-2000	Brown-2800
Over All Words:				
Maximum (syllables)	6	6	8	6
Average (syllables)	2.01	1.85	2.74	1.97
Median (syllables)	1	2	3	2
Percent monosyllabic	36.8	44.3	11.5	39.1
Over Confused Words Only:				
Maximum (syllables)	3	2	2	3
Average (syllables)	1.19	1.05	1.35	1.2
Median (syllables)	1	1	1	1
Percent monosyllabic	82.5	95.3	65.0	82.2

correlation between word frequency and length; the lack of confusability might be a property of long words. Alternatively, confusability might be a property of function words, as opposed to content words. An examination of monosyllabic words helps to decide between these accounts.

We observed that monosyllabic words have the greatest potential for lexical confusions, as opposed to function words *per se* (see Table 4.2). Whereas the median length of words in the uncommon-2000 set is three syllables, the median length of confusable words in this dictionary is only one. In fact, the median length in syllables of those words confused with at least one other word is one in all cases. This shows that monosyllabic words, even low-frequency ones and not just short, high-frequency words, have the highest potential for confusions.

We also looked at sequences of words which could be confused with a given word. For example, "almost" is identical to "all" + "most". In addition, we relaxed the condition that the right boundary of a word must align with the right boundary of a word sequence. For instance, the word "ambiguous" could be heard as the words "am," "big," "you" followed by the beginning of the word "assume" —[əs] (see Figure 4.1).

'Cause I'm big you assume I'm a Texan

am big you assume

ambiguous

FIGURE 4.1 Word containment (garden paths)

TABLE 4.3
How Many Words Are There in Each Word of sx-1800?

# OF WORDS	SAME P-SYMBOL AT RIGHT EDGE	SAME SYLLABLE AT RIGHT EDGE	SAME FOOT AT RIGHT EDGE
Maximum	2322	64	28
Average	51.51	3.15	2.58
Median	4	1	1
Total word overlap	505 (28.20%)	302 (16.86%)	124 (6.92%)

In Figure 4.1, there is what we term a one syllable *overlap* between the last part of the word 'ambiguous' and the first part of the word 'assume.' We experimented with overlap of a single dictionary symbol, a syllable, and a foot for all combinations of all words in the wordlist to give us some measure of the problem of lexical access in continuous speech (see Table 4.3). Longer units, such as syllables or feet, as opposed to single sounds, exhibit less overlap and appear to be useful in limiting search, given, for example, a hashing scheme where these units are encoded in a large dictionary. Harrington and Johnstone (1987, p. 282) advocate a somewhat similar idea in terms of a chart parser: "only those matching words which are greater than two phonemes in length are stored [first] on the word lattice." However, with a fixed-length, longest-first strategy, search will be limited but correct words will be missed entirely. Problems with such filtering schemes are discussed in Harrington and Johnstone.[4]

In conclusion, we found that for a modest vocabulary, lexical confusion does not appear to be particularly severe if word boundaries are known, as in the case of isolated word recognition. This held true even when we compared over 180,000 variant forms. The problem is worse when at least one boundary is not known. It also appeared that monosyllabic words, and not just high-frequency short words, have the greatest potential for inter-word confusion when various pronunciations are permitted. This result may seem surprising to both psycholinguists and automatic speech recognition system builders. Two considerations may clarify the finding. First, in any given sentence, function words undergo reduction processes more often than content words. While it is possible to find similar numbers of types of variants for monosyllabic content and function words, the number of tokens of each type is greater for function words; thus one is more likely to observe function word errors for

---

[4] Also of interest, Harrington and Johnstone observe that broad-class representations of a 4,000 word lexicon yield 10 million word strings. We will turn to a discussion of broad class features immediately below.

any given sentence. Second, monosyllabic confusions of content words might appear to be more rare in automatic speech recognition systems because of either the size of the vocabulary or the lack of resemblance between baseforms. For instance, tasks which incorporate alphanumerics into the recognition system are difficult because multiple pairs such as /pi/, /bi/, /di/ are encountered which differ only by one, often similar, sound and hence are highly confusable, and worse, are themselves contained in polysyllabic words. In such difficult domains, it is common either to make the vocabulary be small or to request that speakers pause between words. In the case of speech perception, semantic and pragmatic factors aid in lexical disambiguation. So one is only faced with the monosyllabic word problem in technology that seeks to recognize very large vocabulary, natural speech where one cannot realistically expect to model critical semantic and pragmatic knowledge.

4.2.2 Implications for cohort speech recognition models

A novel approach to applying cohort theory to speech recognition was developed by researchers who advocated a two-pass word identification strategy (Shipman and Zue 1982; Chen 1985; Huttenlocher and Zue 1983; Huttenlocher 1985). These researchers recommended a fast initial recognition stage based on easily identifiable, "coarse" features in the signal which would yield one or more cohorts of candidate items. A second, more computationally expensive, pass would distinguish among the candidates in a cohort.

Carter (1987) offers criticism of the emphasis on coarse (or "broad") manner features in the two-pass word identification studies, claiming that, when analyzed correctly, the stress pattern and the number of segments in a word contribute half of the work in forming word cohorts. Looking at the interrelated nature of manner, stress and number of phonemes, Carter goes on to conclude:

> ... if only a manner of articulation transcription is to be used, then it is just as important to have that transcription for unstressed syllables as for stressed. Thus either we can concentrate on extracting manner information, *or* we can concentrate on stressed syllables, but if we do both together then the relative informativeness of stressed syllables disappears (Carter 1987, p. 9).

As we alluded to when outlining Luce's 1986 study, we find it premature to accept any claim based on quantitative measures of cohort size using simple pronunciation lists, including Carter's claim just cited. Although such studies pose important questions, we hope that the reader is by now convinced that speakers do more to the pronunciation of words than to collapse manner or class, and that speakers do not keep stress and the number of segments in a word constant, and therefore, that the data that are quantified in cohort studies represent crude approximations. Thus ideas regarding the utility of manner, stress, or other features have not yet been disproven, nor have such features been conclusively demonstrated to be a central mechanism in actual speech perception.

4.3 Stability

The fact that we could model the TIMIT pronunciations in the PPS using simple unordered rule statements led us to ask: (1) what are the key sources of generated variation in the rules; and (2) how can we be sure that we are using a reasonable set of context descriptions in the model?

4.3.1 Where do the rules apply in a word?

There was a total of roughly 350,000 rules applications in the TIMIT-1800 word list; 265,000 in the Brown-1800; and 425,000 in the Brown-2800. There were approximately three hundred rules in the set that was used in the PPS. Subtracting the rules that proved inapplicable to these various word lists, each of the remaining rules applied an average of 1450 times. Thus, the total rule set was applied on average somewhat less than once per word. This number is more meaningful than the number of rules in a set. For instance, the statement

("æ" "ɨ" (:unstressed (:before "n" "d" "t")))   "advance"

can easily be formulated as one, two or three rules, depending on the use of disjunctive or, distinctive features, or bracketing conventions, or it might be collapsed with yet another rule. The number of transformations is the more revealing figure.

In the TIMIT-1800 run, the number of transformations to the dictionary baseforms, as opposed to derived forms, was 23,225, or about one-fifteenth of all applications. Table 4.4 shows the high number of applications to unstressed elements. There were 350,031 rule applications using the TIMIT-1800 words. In contrast, only 263,287 rule applications were observed in the 1800 word list composed of the most frequent items in the Brown corpus. In that run, the contextual environment of 32 rules was never met, as opposed to 25 rules for the TIMIT-1800 set. Table 4.4 also shows data from a run on a larger set of words from the Brown corpus. It yielded 420,477 successful rule applications. Of particular interest is the relatively large number of vowel transformations in word-final position, as well as in word-initial position.

The numbers pertaining to vowel position effects leads us to observe more generally that certain portions of a word are more stable than

TABLE 4.4
A Comparison of TIMIT-1800, Brown-1800 and Brown-2800

	# OF APPLICATIONS	CONTEXT DESCRIPTOR	COMMENT
TIMIT-1800	66841	:unstressed	
	54452	:word-initial	4031 baseform cons. transformed
	24512	:word-final	8739 baseform vowels transformed
	23225	:original baseform	
	7705	:stressed	
Brown-1800	57483	:unstressed	
	49681	:word-initial	2615 baseform cons. transformed
	15885	:word-final	8139 baseform vowels transformed
	18449	:original baseform	
	5787	:stressed	
Brown-2800	90791	:unstressed	
	73157	:word-initial	4955 baseform cons. transformed
	27657	:word-final	11118 baseform vowels transformed
	28516	:original baseform	
	10317	:stressed	

others, and that presumably, more informative for purposes of word discrimination. To illustrate this, we ran the unordered rule component on disyllabic words. In Table 4.5, the degree of variability reflects the total rule application, so that units annotated with "most variable" are those where most rules can apply. The table highlights the roles of stress and word and syllable position on the degree of variability of pronunciation. Where a word is likely to remain stable is an important issue for a theory of lexical access.

An examination of the distribution of the rule applications in our model reveals that certain rules apply much more frequently than others, and that there are several asymmetries in rule application. In the experiment using the TIMIT-1800 word list, 66,800 rule applications were in unstressed environments while 7,700 were in stressed environments. While the ratio of the number of rules which specify unstressed as opposed to stressed contextual environments is 2:1 in the PPS, the ratio of the observed number of applications is 8:1. Since the word list consists largely of disyllabic and monosyllabic words, this indicates that there is a feeding effect in unstressed syllables, so that changes in these syllables license further changes, which means that unstressed syllables are variable indeed.

Of interest also is word-initial position, which showed 54,500 rule applications. Of these, only 4050 applications were to word-initial consonants, which means that word-initial vowels are predicted to be highly

TABLE 4.5
What Portion of a Word is Most Variable?

	[Consonant	Vowel]	[Consonant	Vowel	Consonant]	Example
1.	[C+stress	V+stress]	[C variable	V variable	C] most variable	*rallied*
2.	[C+stress	V+stress]	[C variable	V] variable		*Raleigh*
3.		[V+stress] variable	[C variable	V variable	C] most variable	*Alice*
4.		[V+stress] variable	[C variable	V] variable		*alley*
5.		[V] most variable	[C+stress	V+stress	C+stress] variable	*align*
6.	[C variable	V] variable	[C+stress	V+stress]		*rely*

variable, even if they are in a stressed syllable. In contrast, in the 24,500 applications in word-final position, vowels are transformed less often than consonants, with 8750 applications.

We give in Appendix B a list of confusability cohorts based on the application of the rules.

Because of the astronomical number of pronunciations an ordinary sentence is capable of displaying, it is interesting to consider the hypothesis that the more stable stressed syllables enjoy a special status in recognition (modulo the comment regarding vowel-initial words) and, by the same reasoning, that certain manner features are more stable than either place features or other manner features such as the voicing of elements in certain positions in the word.

In order to fully understand why and when a given word is likely to appear in a perceptual cohort, we must know, first, the likelihood of segmental changes produced by the speaker, and second, the probability that either the dictionary symbol or the transformed phonetic element will be correctly classified by the listener. In the final chapter we turn to the question of estimating the probability that a given phonetic element will be transformed in a given contextual environment.

4.3.2 Limits of confusability

The PPS predicts many perceptual confusions among words from moderate-sized dictionaries. Yet we doubt if people often confuse 'adorn' and 'darn,' or 'litre' and 'lieder', as predicted by our model. As the psychological literature tells us, simple word frequency is one aspect that should be modeled. One of the more interesting possibilities is that of a *dynamic cache*, whereby words recently seen are more likely to be predicted (Kupiec 1989; Hunnicutt 1987; Jelinek 1985).

One set of experiments, conducted by Kupiec, concerned improving the efficiency of word lookup in systems containing very large dictionaries. In such systems dictionary access may be organized in multiple layers. Typically this might involve an extremely large dictionary providing a high degree of coverage, and having a costly access, and a smaller dictionary "cache" containing the more commonly used words, which is less expensive to access. Hunnicutt and colleagues have explored various types of frequency ordered lexicons for word prediction applications, and have implemented a system which allows word frequency to "be temporarily raised during a conversation about a specific topic" (Hunnicutt 1987; see also Kuhn 1988). This is another way to accomplish the effect of a dynamic cache, if the topic of conversation can be analyzed in some fashion. Matching first against a cache of predicted words is useful in any system that does not, or cannot, perform exhaustive search, or one that has little access to distinguishing pragmatic information.

Two methods of organizing the dictionary cache were compared. In one organization the cache simply contained the overall most frequent words occurring in the corpus. The other method consisted of maintaining a dynamically changing vocabulary, composed of the most recent words encountered when scanning the corpus. Results showed that over a wide range of dictionary sizes the coverage provided by the dynamically changing cache was at least as good as that provided by the list of most frequent words. Thus, comparable performance is achieved without any prior analysis of the corpus contents. A further advantage lies in the inherent adaptability of the dynamic organization to unrestricted domains, where the topic may vary greatly.

4.4   Conclusion

Many automatic speech recognition system builders we know jokingly say that given the amount of variability in pronunciation, speech perception succeeds only through mind-reading. Such an appreciation for the difficulty of decoding speech surfaces as syntactic and pragmatic constraints in software and as a form of stability (island-of-certainty schemes) in algorithms. It is interesting to observe that hidden Markov modeling (HMM) systems automatically embed the island-of-certainty notion in the local branching factor of the network: in our terminology, the most stable regions have the fewest transitions.

Because the kind of variability we observe in ordinary American speech implicates rich language structure, one might expect recognition systems to make use of metrical units. Yet they don't. In a similar vein, pronunciation nets are often constructed ignoring levels of structure beyond linear sequences of phones. The central reason for not using metrical structure in spoken language applications, we suggest, follows from the relative lack of careful studies aimed at quantifying the effect of prosodic environments on the realization of speech sounds, stemming in part from the lack of data for simultaneously analyzing segmental and prosodic environments. It is known that phones do not appear simply in free variation, but that they vary in context.

In our work, we asked under what circumstances phonetic variation is conditioned, and what context descriptions best describe the variation, from a quantitative as well as qualitative perspective. We found specifiable subsets of phonetic contexts that limit overgeneration, and moreover that the context descriptions account for all but largely aberrant pronunciations observed in the transcribed sentences. The enriched set of context descriptors was adequate to fuel the PPS for generating the pronunciations observed in the data without using hand-determined rule-ordering to limit overgeneration.

We now turn to a new methodology for automatically creating metrically enriched rules and pronunciation networks for recognition systems given a training corpus and a set of theoretically and empirically motivated context descriptors.

5

Statistical modeling of phonological variation

Most current speech recognition systems model words with a single pronunciation or a small number of alternate pronunciations. For systems which use statistical training of models of speech segments, this lack of explicit representation of the range of variation of pronunciation causes different phenomena to be averaged together into the same model, resulting in a less precise model. (SRI's DECIPHER System, Murveit et al. 1989, p. 239.)

As observed in previous chapters, the lexical context in which a dictionary symbol occurs leads to consistent differences in how it is pronounced. A variety of *contextual descriptors*, or *contextual factors*, such as syllable stress and syllable boundaries, can be used to account for these phonological variants. These descriptors are derived from units and features for which there exist good cross-linguistic evidence in the phonologies of the world's languages.

However, there are two interrelated difficulties in the use of these descriptors for applications such as speech recognition and synthesis. First, not all variation can be uniquely predicted based on contextual descriptors, because speech is inherently variable. Consequently, different linguistic phenomena may occur in the same context. For example, both the unaspirated and aspirated variants of /t/ may occur in the phrase 'not many'. But we also know that the /t/ in 'not many' is more likely to be unaspirated than aspirated. Therefore, given a set of examples, the relative frequency or probability of each variant occurring in a given context can be estimated by using statistical methods, resulting in greater descriptive adequacy in characterizing when different

This chapter is based in part on "Identification of Contextual Factors for Pronunciation Networks," which appeared in *Proceedings of the 1990 International Conference on Acoustics, Speech, and Signal Processing*; Albuquerque, NM, April 3–6, 1990; pp. 753–56. ©1990 IEEE.

phenomena occur. For some applications, phonological information is more valuable if, rather than just predicting what is possible, there is also information about the likelihood of each possibility. Quantification of such information is useful for speech recognition systems for building word models. It is also potentially useful for speech synthesis systems in adding variability in order to produce more natural sounding speech.

The second difficulty is that one may want to know which context descriptions best model a particular language behavior. In traditional studies, so-called "crucial examples" are sought in deciding between possible rival accounts. In practice, there prove to be many accounts of linguistic phenomena, even when given a well-defined set of descriptive units. From a set of data, one can define the "best" model to be the model which is best in terms of predicting the behavior of new data. But with a moderate number of descriptors, finding the best combination of descriptors is usually computationally prohibitive. Nevertheless, a "good" model can be found which is optimal in a local sense and which systematically selects a set of context descriptors based on a large number of examples.

In this chapter, a data-intensive method for building "good" statistical models for predicting variation in pronunciation is described. Also discussed is use of the models to build statistically-based *pronunciation networks* which can capture many types of contextual effects. First, motivation is provided for the underlying baseform representation with an enriched set of contextual descriptors. Next, a method is described for automatically identifying subsets of contextual factors which, taken together, are useful for predicting phonological variation. This method organizes the contextual descriptions into mutually exclusive subsets represented as a *context tree*. In particular, one context tree is created for each dictionary symbol. The tree representation enables categorization of different pronunciations of a dictionary symbol according to the context in which they appear in the corpus, as well as permitting quantification of phonological phenomena. In addition, this representation is amenable to simplifications leading to parsimonious descriptions of the context under which the variant pronunciations occur. The context descriptions in a tree are composed of mixed, or different subsets of, contextual factors. By using mixed contextual descriptors, a small number of factors are used to describe each phonological phenomena, but globally, for all observed phenomena, the total number of factors encoded in a tree may be large.

The information in a context tree can be used to predict the pronunciation of a dictionary symbol in any given context. In the last part of this chapter, the creation of pronunciation networks using the information in a set of context trees is presented. The set of trees is composed of one tree for each dictionary symbol, plus one tree describing when insertions occur. Given the dictionary baseform of a word, a network is automatically derived from the context tree information. Each such network compactly describes phonetic variation in a word and can be joined with other word networks to create sentences and phrases.

5.1 Pronunciation models in speech recognition systems

A primary application of phonological modeling is building pronunciation models for speech recognition systems. Although many of the pronunciation models developed by researchers in speech recognition are context-dependent, only a limited number of contexts are generally used. This is due in part to the need to train speech recognition systems on a large amount of data.[1] With a larger number of contexts, more data are required for training because of the larger number of parameters which must be estimated. Empirical experiments, such as those described below, demonstrate that better modeling of phonological variation through the use of a wider variety of contexts can improve the performance of speech recognition systems.

The simplest phone-based pronunciation model is context-free and is sometimes referred to as a *monophone model*. Bahl *et al.* (1980) introduced a simple context-dependent model, known as a *triphone model*, which accounts for contextual effects of adjacent phones. Triphones can be concatenated to create model words, thus providing easy additions to the lexicon; however, triphones account for only a subset of contextual factors. Triphone models have been found to be better models than monophones (*e.g.*, Chow *et al.* 1986) and are used now by many recognition systems. Lee (see Lee 1988; Lee *et al.* 1989) introduced the ideas of generalized triphones and clustered triphones, in which triphones exhibiting similar behavior (due to coarticulation) are grouped together. Because of the smaller number of models, generalized triphones and clustered triphones are better trained for a given amount of training data. *Whole-word models*, where phones may be represented in the context of the word in which they occur (*e.g.*, Paul and Martin 1988; Bahl *et al.* 1979), provide the most complete context of the internal phones, but usually do not model word boundary effects well. This is because

---

[1]Mercer (1988) observed that by increasing the amount of data used to develop the language model in IBM's speech recognition system, the error rate was reduced. He summarized this finding with the phrase: "There's no data like more data." Many researchers have since observed that this phrase applies when training a speaker-independent speech recognition system(*e.g.*, Lee *et al.* 1989; Paul 1990), and it has become somewhat of a slogan.

examples of each word in each possible context would be needed to create models which are context-independent at word boundaries.

Paul (1988) has conducted studies comparing the recognition rates of whole-word models, triphone models, and monophone models. In his work, he found that whole-word models provided somewhat better recognition rates over triphone models, and that triphone models have much better recognition rates than monophone models. However, in these studies, context across word boundaries was not modeled. Several researchers (Paul 1989; Weintraub *et al.* 1989; Lee *et al.* 1989) have observed that use of *cross-word triphone models*, that is, triphone models which apply across word boundaries, provided significantly better recognition rates over word-internal triphone models. Extrapolating, one would expect even better performance with whole-word models which also modeled contextual effects across word boundaries. However, the amount of data necessary to train whole-word models for a moderate size vocabulary can be prohibitive. The addition of a new word to the vocabulary of a system which uses whole-word context-dependent models would require many new tokens of the word because at least one token of the word in each context in which it could appear would be required.

Instead of words, smaller representational units, such as phones, with an enriched set of contextual descriptors, can provide models which capture many of the same contextual effects as whole-word models, without the disadvantage of requiring training data for each new word added the vocabulary. Phone models are generally used in speech recognition systems, in part because models for new words can be created from previously trained phone models, and smoothing techniques for estimating distributions (Jelinek and Mercer 1980) can be used when only a small amount of training data is available.

By using a wide variety of contextual factors, more contextual effects are captured, and predictions of pronunciation variants are modeled better. In turn, the models can be encoded into pronunciation networks and used in speech recognition systems to improve their performance. A case in point is the work by Weintraub *et al.* (1989) who found that phonological modeling improved their recognition results. In their work, the phonological rules were derived by hand but trained automatically.

A final argument for the use of a larger number of contexts is based on the work of Hogg and Kephart (1988), who describe a general theory of categorization tasks with a large number of features. In their work they show that a sub-optimal method based on many features can work as well as a perfect method based on a few features. In this work, we increase the number of features, or contextual factors, used to predict phonological variation by using a locally optimal algorithm for selecting a subset of the factors, dependent on the data, such that locally a small number of factors are used, but globally a large number of factors are in effect used.

5.2 Representation of context

In this section we propose the use of a metrically-enriched underlying representation for modeling surface phonetic variation. This representation permits the addition of new words to the vocabulary without additional training data, as would be needed for whole-word models. This representation also allows us to capture long-range contextual effects such as contextual factors which extend over syllables and across word boundaries. In representing contexts for describing phonological variation, the desire to use a variety of contextual factors is opposed by the finite amount of data available for modeling. We show how our representation and the use of data-derived context trees allow us to accommodate both criteria.

5.2.1 Contextual factors

In this chapter, as in Chapter 3, we examine variation in the pronunciation of spoken words, relative to the baseforms given in a dictionary. In contrast to the earlier study, here we use a statistically-based approach which permits the likelihood of the different variant pronunciations to be estimated, based on similarities in contextual influence on observed phonetic realization. As described earlier, we refer to the dictionary pronunciation symbols as *dictionary symbols*. The various pronunciations of a dictionary symbol, or *phonetic elements*, are derived from transcriptions of speech and are represented by a set of transcription symbols.

As in the pronunciation generation and log-linear studies described in Chapter 3, the *mappings* were derived by comparing transcriptions of spoken speech with a dictionary representation of the words spoken. The *X-dictionary* (see Section 2.1.1) was used, and the transcriptions were taken from almost 30,000 hand-transcribed segments in approximately 900 of the "sx" sentences from the TIMIT database. As before, our primary interest is the type of acoustic element observed, and pronunciations are represented using phonetic elements. To apply the results of this study to the creation of a pronunciation network for a speech recognition system, each phonetic element that represents two TIMIT phones, such as an aspirated plosive that represents a closure and a release, are converted back into the original two TIMIT phones to model the two acoustically distinct regions.

We describe the context of a dictionary symbol, and the mapping

TABLE 5.1
Contextual Factors Used in Pronunciation Studies

Contextual Factor	Values
preceding-dictionary-symbol	(all dictionary symbols) + sentence-boundary
following-dictionary-symbol	(all dictionary symbols) + sentence-boundary
preceding-phonetic-element	(all phonetic elements) + deletion + sentence-boundary
following-phonetic-element	(all phonetic elements) + deletion + sentence-boundary
syllable-part	onset, nucleus, coda
stress	primary, secondary, unstressed
syllable-boundary-type	initial, final, not-initial-not-final, initial-and-final
foot-boundary-type	initial, final, not-initial-not-final, initial-and-final
word-boundary-type	initial, final, not-initial-not-final, initial-and-final
cluster-type	onset, coda, nil
open-syllable?	true, false
true-vowel?	true, false
function word?	true, false

from a dictionary symbol to phonetic element, using many types of linguistically motivated *contextual factors*, such as stress and word-boundary-type. Each contextual factor describing the context of a dictionary symbol has a *value*. For example, the factor stress may take on any one value of primary, secondary, or unstressed. The factors used in this study are derived from the set used by the pronunciation generation system described in Chapter 4. These factors and associated values are listed in Table 5.1. Additional factors could easily be added into the model, with the primary penalty being additional computational requirements. Each of these factors, except for preceding-phonetic-element and following-phonetic-element, describes a lexical context. We chose to use lexical descriptors, rather than features from the speech signal, because lexical descriptors provide a simple context description without ambiguity. For example, *lexical* stress can be looked up in a dictionary, whereas *acoustical* stress is not as easily determined since it is computed from the signal. In addition, most lexical descriptors, such as foot-boundary-type, do not always have a clear acoustic correlate.

Each of the contextual factors defines a separate dimension. As a consequence, the values of a factor are defined independently from irrelevant linguistic structures. For example, the context values based on adjacent dictionary symbols are defined across word boundaries. In the phrase 'two words', the value of following-dictionary-symbol for /u/ in 'two' is the /w/ in 'words'.

Some of the factors listed in Table 5.1 are derived from structures normally associated with several dictionary symbols. For example, the factor syllable-part may take on the value onset, which may be composed of up to three dictionary symbols, as in the sequence /str/. In such cases, we assign the factor value to each dictionary symbol within the structure. In this example, the tokens /s/, /t/, and /r/ in an /str/ sequence would each be assigned a syllable-part value of onset. This representation allows modeling of long-range contextual effects simultaneously with a local representation, which simplifies the addition of new words to a recognition vocabulary.

The values of a contextual factor were defined such that the factor space is partitioned into mutually exclusive subspaces. For example, the factor syllable-boundary-type has the values: initial (and not final), final (and not initial), not-initial-not-final and initial-and-final. Predicates can be explicitly defined by grouping the values of a contextual factor. Thus, the predicate syllable-initial? is formed when the values of syllable-boundary-type are clustered into the two groups {initial, initial-and-final} and {final, not-initial-and-not-final}.

If the context of a dictionary symbol is described by simultaneously using all the contextual factors listed in Table 5.1, a prohibitive amount of data would be required to form an adequate description of each dictionary symbol in each context. Each contextual factor represents a separate dimension, and with such a large number of dimensions, the distribution of dictionary symbols in a context will be sparse. One way to handle this difficulty is to build a *decision tree*, in which a subset of contextual factors are selected using a greedy algorithm[2] which minimizes the loss of information at each selection. (A type of decision tree, called a *context tree*, will be introduced in the next section.) An alternate method for selecting contextual factors, based on "binary splitting of subspaces" until a preset number of "clusters" is formed, is given by Sagayama (1989). In Sagayama's method, a tree is grown to a preset number of terminal nodes, and only binary splits of the values of a contextual factor are allowed.

Recently, several researchers have used decision trees for predicting

---

[2]In a *greedy* algorithm, locally optimal decisions are made at each step, but the result may not be globally optimal.

TABLE 5.2
Contextual Factors for the Planting Example

CONTEXTUAL FACTOR	VALUES
windy	yes, no
humidity	high, normal
sky	sunny, overcast, rain
temperature	hot, mild, cool
phase of moon	new, full, 1st quarter, 3rd quarter

pronunciations. The triphone clustering work by Lee (1988) considered only contexts described by adjacent phones. This work was motivated by the idea that one of the primary influences on the pronunciation of sounds in a word is the surrounding dictionary symbols and that the large number of possible phone combinations might be reduced by grouping similarly influenced phones. In subsequent work, researchers considered a larger number of contexts. These works take an approach based on using decision trees to select a subset of contextual factors for predicting the various ways of pronouncing a dictionary symbol. Bahl *et al.* (1991) have created phone pronunciation models as a function of the five preceding and five following phones. They have tested these models in a recognition system and found that recognition performance improved. Lee *et al.* (1990) clustered allophones based on a set of pre-defined linguistically-motivated contextual factors, and reported that it led to high performance recognition. Riley (1989) has also looked at statistically estimating phoneme to phone mappings, in which one tree for all phones is constructed, rather than constructing a separate tree for each phone, as in the other studies.

In each of these works, binary "questions" or branching of the data is performed. However, an "understandable" division of contextual factor values is not always binary. Following Chen and Shrager (1989) and Chen (1990), we next describe how a decision tree can be created in which the number of groups of contextual factor values is determined from the data. This type of tree is called a *context tree*. We begin by briefly outlining how a decision tree is created.

5.3 Context trees

A context tree is an n-ary decision tree which provides a representation for modeling the relationship between contextual factors and the variant pronunciations of a dictionary symbol in different contexts. Decision trees have been used for both interpretation and classification of data (Payne and Meisel 1977; Henrichon and Fu 1969). Given a data

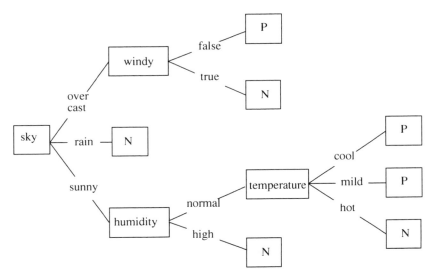

FIGURE 5.1 Decision tree for the planting example

set, decision trees partition the data set and can be formed automatically (Breiman *et al.* 1984; Quinlan 1986). The resulting trees can be converted to rules (Quinlan 1987), which is convenient if one wishes to analyze the phonological rules encoded in a tree or compare them with a hand-derived set of rules.

5.3.1 A brief look at decision trees

Many statistical techniques depend upon a linear relationship between the "stimulus" and "response," or in our case, between the contextual factors including the dictionary baseform and the predicted phonetic element. When such an assumption is not correct, a decision tree may be a better model. In creating a decision tree, many contextual factors which are not relevant to predicting the response are automatically separated from relevant predictors. As a simple example, a decision tree similar to one given in Quinlan 1987 can be used to answer the question: Should the garden be planted today? Several contextual factors which might be relevant are shown in Table 5.2. Also illustrated are several possible values for each of the contextual factors. For example, the contextual factor **sky** has three values: **sunny**, **overcast**, and **rain**. An example of a Quinlan-style decision tree is shown in Figure 5.1. The box labeled **sky** is the *root node* and the boxes labeled N or P are *terminal nodes*, corresponding to negative and positive outcomes, respectively.

TABLE 5.3
Sample Training Set for the Planting Example

TOKEN NO.	ATTRIBUTES					CLASS
	Sky	*Temp.*	*Humidity*	*Windy*	*Moon Phase*	
1	rain	hot	high	false	new	N
2	rain	hot	high	true	full	N
3	overcast	hot	high	false	new	P
4	rain	mild	high	false	1st	N
5	sunny	hot	normal	false	3rd	N
6	rain	cool	normal	true	1st	N
7	overcast	cool	normal	true	full	N
8	sunny	mild	high	false	3rd	N
9	sunny	cool	normal	false	new	P
10	sunny	mild	normal	false	1st	P
11	sunny	mild	normal	true	3rd	P
12	overcast	mild	high	true	full	N
13	overcast	hot	normal	false	new	P
14	rain	mild	high	true	new	N

At each of the non-terminal nodes a question is asked about the value of the contextual factor associated with the node. For example, the root node represents the contextual factor sky, which has three possible answers: overcast, rain, or sunny. Each answer is represented on a separate branch from the node. Depending on the answer, another question may be asked. If the answer is overcast, then the question of whether it is windy is asked. For a particular set of planting conditions, the predicted outcome is computed by starting at the root node of the tree and following a path corresponding to the values of the planting conditions. Note that in this tree, the contextual factor phase of moon was not found to be relevant.

To compute a decision tree, a set of labeled tokens, or *training set*, is needed. One such set that could be used to create a tree to determine whether or not to plant the garden today is shown in Table 5.3. From the labeled tokens, relations between contextual factor values and class are noted and strong predictors of a class are selected to create the decision tree. This will be discussed in more detail in Section 5.3.3.

5.3.2 Computation of context trees

In this section our method for automatically constructing decision trees which are appropriate for organizing the values of contextual factors and the phonetic mapping of a dictionary symbol is described. These decision trees, which we refer to as context trees, select a subset of contextual factors and provide a compact representation of the relationship

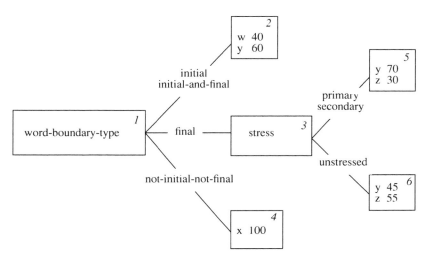

FIGURE 5.2 Context tree. Node numbers are in the
upper right corner of a box.

between a context and the phonetic elements observed in the context.
A context tree also models the fact that the probability of a phonetic
realization varies with the context in which the dictionary symbol occurs. These trees may be used for the construction of pronunciation
rules and for predicting phonetic elements from a dictionary symbol in
context. In constructing context trees, a set of training tokens is used.
The values of a contextual factor which similarly influence the pronunciation realizations of a dictionary symbol are grouped based on similarity
in phonetic element *distributions* observed in the training data. These
groups of factor values form descriptive categories which often resemble
theoretical categories or features, such as vocalic or plosive, and define
the organization of the tree.

As in the planting example, a context tree is used for classification
and prediction by asking a question at each non-terminal node. An illustrative tree is shown in figure 5.2. Each non-terminal node of a context
tree is labeled with a *contextual factor*. In the figure, node 1 corresponds
to the contextual factor **word-boundary-type**. The branches from a node
are labeled with mutually exclusive sets of *values* of the contextual factor and each branch leads from the *parent* node to a *child* node. The
top branch of node 1 represents the values **initial** and **initial-and-final** of
the factor **word-boundary-type**. The middle branch corresponds to the
mutually exclusive value **final**. The context of a terminal node is defined

by the contextual factor values encountered in traversing the tree from the root node to reach the terminal node. For example, terminal node 5 in the figure represents the context word-final with primary or secondary stress. Each terminal node of a context tree encodes the distribution of phonetic elements in each context. In general, more than one phonetic element occurs in a context because realizations of a dictionary symbol are not deterministic. Rather than predicting only the most likely phonetic element in a context, the probability of each of the different possible phonetic elements is enumerated. For example, in the context represented by terminal node 5, the dictionary symbol is predicted to be pronounced as the phonetic element [y] 70% of the time and as [z] 30% of the time.

Three characteristics of speech are accommodated by our tree representation:

1. A dictionary symbol can be pronounced in multiple ways.
2. The number of values for some contextual factors may be large. For example, the context preceding-dictionary-symbol has 46 values in our dictionary's alphabet. Splitting the data based on all 46 values rapidly decreases the number of tokens per node.
3. The appropriate number of groups of values is not always binary; for example, there are more than two places of articulation.

These three characteristics of speech are accommodated through the use of tree induction and clustering of context values, which are described in the next two sections.

5.3.3 Selection of contextual factors by tree induction

A decision tree is built by recursively splitting the data in a parent node into subsets which form descendant, or child, nodes. To split the data at a node, the "best" contextual factor is selected. One child node is created for each value of the selected factor. Then each token in the current node is assigned to one of the child nodes based on the token's value of the selected factor. The method of tree induction described is adapted from the decision tree induction method of ID3 (Quinlan 1986).

The "best" contextual factor at each node is defined to be the factor which best separates the different realizations of a dictionary symbol when the data are split based on the factor's values. This results in the greatest reduction in the uncertainty about the probability of occurrence of each phonetic element and may be computed based on a statistical measure known as *entropy*. Entropy can be thought of as a measure of the "randomness" in a set of tokens, such as the distribution of phonetic elements in a node. Thus, entropy may be used as a measure of how well a contextual factor separates the phonetic elements associated with the data in a node. As a context tree is induced, the entropy of the tree is reduced by creating purer child nodes.[3] That is, as a tree is grown, the uncertainty about the probability of occurrence of each phonetic element in the different contexts is reduced. A more formal working description of the use of entropy for measuring the purity of the nodes of a context tree is briefly reviewed here (for a more detailed treatment, see Breiman *et al.* 1984; Chou 1988; Gallager 1968; or Ganapathy and Rajaraman 1973).

Let the entropy at a node based on the phonetic elements A be $H(A)$:

$$H(A) = -\sum_a P(a) log P(a)$$

where $P(a)$ is the probability of the phonetic element a occurring and $\{a\}$ represents all possible phonetic elements A. After splitting the data in a node according to the values V of a given contextual factor, the average entropy of the phonetic elements in the new nodes, $E(H(A|v))$, is:

$$E(H(A|v)) = \sum_v P(v) H(A|v)$$

where $\{v\}$ represents all possible values V of the contextual factor and $E()$ is the expected value. The average entropy can also be expressed as the conditional entropy of phonetic element A given factor values V, or $H(A|V)$. The gain, or increase in purity, for contextual factor f, $G(f)$, is the difference between the entropy of the phonetic elements at a node, $H(A)$, and the conditional entropy of the phonetic elements A, given the data at a node has been split into child nodes based on the values V. $G(f)$ may also be expressed as the *average mutual information* between A and V, $I(A;V)$:

$$G(f) = H(A) - H(A|V) = I(A;V).$$

The average entropy can be reduced by splitting the data into a greater number of child nodes such that with enough child nodes, each node is pure. In general, as the number of splits increases, the average entropy of the child nodes tends to decrease. Since the data are split based on the number of factor values, which vary with each factor, the gain for factor f is normalized by the entropy of the number of values associated with f, $H(V)$. Quinlan calls this the *gain ratio*, $R(f)$:

$$R(f) = G(f)/H(V).$$

At each non-terminal node, the factor which maximizes the gain ratio is selected for splitting.

---

[3]A *pure* node contains tokens of only one realization type.

The entropy measure attempts to segregate all phonetic elements simultaneously. Consequently, the contextual factors selected to predict when a dictionary symbol will be mapped to one particular phonetic element may be different than those selected to predict when a dictionary symbol will be mapped to each of the possible phonetic element mappings. For example, to identify when /t/ glottalization occurs, the phonetic elements of /t/ are encoded as glottalized and not-glottalized in the data used to build the context tree. The resulting tree will contain a specific set of contextual factors pertinent only to glottalization. In contrast, to identify the contexts under which the different phonetic elements of /t/ occur, a set of contextual factors pertinent to *simultaneously* differentiating among all the phonetic elements will be selected. Thus one advantage of this methodology over individual rule creation is that the *global* usefulness of each attribute in separating the different phonetic elements is considered as the trees are constructed.

This section has described a statistically-based algorithm for identifying the best contextual factor for splitting the data at a node. In the next section, the clustering procedure which groups context values with similar phonetic element distributions to form categories is discussed.

5.3.4 Clustering of contextual factor values

Traditionally, in tree induction, the data in a node are split either on *all* values of a factor (*e.g.*, Quinlan 1986) or else a *binary* split is used (*e.g.*, Breiman *et al.* 1984). However, splitting the data in a node based on *general classes* may be more suitable for speech pronunciation data. Splitting on all values of a factor does not allow for the fact that some of the individual values influence the pronunciation of a dictionary symbol in a similar way. Also, on a practical note, some factors, such as preceding-dictionary-symbol, have many different values, and splitting the data along all values would rapidly reduce the number of tokens per node. Hence, rather than splitting the data on all values of a factor, it is desirable to group the values of a factor with similar effects into general classes and then split the data based on the general classes.

To determine the general classes, the values could be pre-clustered by hand according to theoretical ideas of what is similar. This is a labor-intensive task since the groupings may change from one context to another. For example, the values of the factor preceding-dictionary-symbol could be grouped based on *manner* of articulation. Such a grouping is useful when predicting the pronunciation of a plosive (*e.g.*, aspirated, unaspirated, flapped, glottalized), but such a grouping is not useful in predicting when /s/ will be palatalized, which is better described by a grouping corresponding to *place* of articulation. Alternatively, the values could be clustered into a predefined number of groups at each node (Chou 1988). However, the appropriate number of groups is not the same for all sounds and again may depend on the current context (*e.g.*, when manner versus place of articulation is applicable). Thus, we want to cluster the values of each factor at a node, and we want the number of clusters to be determined by the tokens in the node. The factor values within each resulting group will then be similar in their prediction of the distribution of phonetic elements. Because more than two general classes sometimes occur (*e.g.*, the possible values of place of articulation), especially when trying to classify more than two types of outcomes, a binary split is not always appropriate.

To group the values of a factor which have a similar effect on the realization of a dictionary symbol, *agglomerative clustering* is used. This type of clustering allows the number of clusters for each set of factor values to be determined from the data, rather than using a set of predefined factor values. Average mutual information is used as the distance metric and is computed as in Jelinek 1985. That is, let the average mutual information, $I(v_i; A)$ between context value v_i and the phonetic elements A be:

$$I(v_i; A) = \sum_a P(v_i, a) log \frac{P(a|v_i)}{P(a)}$$

where $\{a\}$ is composed of all the possible phonetic elements A. The term $\frac{P(a|v_i)}{P(a)}$ compares the probability of phonetic element a occurring given that the token has value v_i for the selected factor and the probability of phonetic element a occurring without such knowledge. The increase in average mutual information resulting from pairing two factor values v_m and v_n is the difference between the average mutual information resulting from pairing v_m and v_n, $I(v_m \cup v_n; A)$, and the contribution to the average mutual information before pairing v_m and v_n, $I(v_m; A) + I(v_n; A)$:

$$\Delta I(V; A) = I(v_m \cup v_n; A) - I(v_m; A) - I(v_n; A).$$

At each iteration, the pairing that results in the largest increase in mutual information is selected and forms a new cluster. Pairing of clusters is continued until one of the following conditions for stopping is reached:

1. There are only two clusters left;
2. The increase in the mutual information is negative and more than doubles from one iteration to the next; or
3. The increase in the mutual information measure decreases more than a threshold, which was set at -30.

Conditions (2) and (3) were determined empirically. At each iteration, the increase in mutual information is often negative because some information is usually lost each time a new cluster is formed. The conditions for stopping define when the loss in mutual information is so large that clusters containing disparate values would be combined.

Since the values of each factor are clustered prior to splitting, it may be useful to split on a factor several times, each time under a more specific context (*i.e.*, farther down the tree). Thus, in contrast to Quinlan's method, after a factor is selected for splitting, it is *not* removed from the set of factors considered. This is also the case in the binary split method of Breiman *et al.* (1984); however, our method has the potential of splitting phonetic elements into a small, appropriate number of categories, such as in the place of articulation example.

5.3.5 Creation of robust trees

The data used to construct a context tree reflect both systematic influences and random variation, or noise. As a tree is grown using the method described above, the amount of data available at the new nonterminal nodes decreases. Consequently, the estimates become poorer, and random variation rather than systematic influences become the predominant effect modeled. When this happens, a context tree is too specialized to the training tokens and would not be robust with respect to new data. In the extreme case, each terminal node of the tree is pure. To understand the relationship between contexts and phonetic realizations, we need to uncover the systematic influences; this can be achieved by pruning, which combines subtrees, resulting in more general predictions. Many methods of pruning have been suggested (*e.g.*, Breiman *et al.* 1984; Chou 1988), but in general, their primary goal is to minimize the probability of error versus some characteristic of the tree, such as expected path length or number of terminal nodes.

Since our objective is to use only the parts of the tree modeling systematic influences, which should therefore be robust to new data, a different type of pruning was used. A node is extended only when the number of tokens at that node is greater than a specified threshold, as in Breiman *et al.* (1984); we used 20. In addition, only nodes relevant to the classification of tokens are kept, as measured by a chi-square test at the .01 level of significance. This was tested using the following statistic, which is approximately chi-square with $V-1$ degrees of freedom (Quinlan 1986):

$$\sum_{v=1}^{V} \sum_{a=1}^{A} \frac{(x_{va} - \overline{x_{va}})^2}{\overline{x_{va}}}.$$

TABLE 5.4

Key to Symbols Used in Figures 5.3 and 5.4 to Represent
Contextual Factor Values From Table 5.1

Contextual Factor Value	Symbol
initial	I
final	F
initial-and-final	I-F
not-initial-not-final	NI-NF
true	T
false	NIL
sentence-boundary-type	–
deletion	NIL

NOTE: Dictionary symbols are defined in Table 2.1 and Table 2.2 in
Chapter 2.

x_{va} represents the number of tokens with value v for the selected contextual factor and phonetic element realization a. $\overline{x_{va}}$ is the average of x_{va} over the factor values and phonetic elements.

Each tree is also pruned by running an independent set of tokens, or *cross-validation* set, through the constructed tree. If the cross-validation tokens in a node indicate that a factor is not relevant to the classification of the tokens in a node, the subtree beginning at the node is collapsed into a terminal node. Trees were induced using 60% of the data; the results that will be described are based on trees pruned using the remaining 40% of the data.

5.3.6 Discussion of context trees

In this section, two context trees illustrate the information represented in the trees produced by our method of combining standard tree induction techniques with clustering of contextual factor values. We describe generalizations which may be made regarding the selected factors, and argue that the use of subsets of factors is more appropriate and results in better models of phonological variation. Finally, the attributes of the context trees which make them amenable for creating pronunciation networks are described.

A sample tree constructed using the combined tree induction and clustering method is shown in Figure 5.3. This tree is for the case of whether or not /t/ is glottalized. The keys to the symbols in the figure are given in Table 2.1 and Table 2.2 in Chapter 2, and Table 5.4 in this chapter. From the figure, it can be observed that glottalization occurs most frequently in the context specified by terminal nodes 3 and 4. The non-terminal nodes of the tree represent the contextual factors selected to describe when /t/ is glottalized. It can be

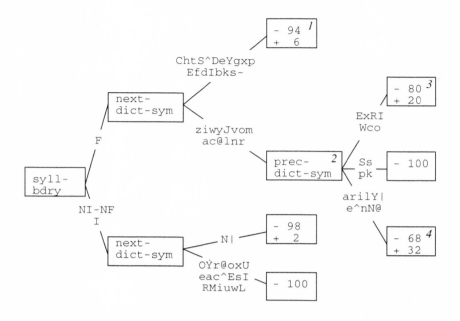

FIGURE 5.3 Pruned tree showing contexts when /t/ is
glottalized (+) and not glottalized (−). Node numbers
are in the upper right corner of a box.

seen that syllable-boundary-type (syll-bdry), following-dictionary symbol (next-dict-sym), and preceding-dictionary-symbol (prec-dict-sym)
were the selected contextual factors. In contrast, the triphone models
commonly employed in speech recognition systems model only the contextual effects of preceding phonetic element (phone) and following phonetic element (phone).

The first split is based on the contextual factor syllable-boundary-
type (syll-bdry), indicating that when /t/ is glottalized, it is generally
in syllable-final position. Note that grouping the syllable-boundary-type
context values not-initial-and-not-final (NI-NF) and initial (I) separately
from final (F) can be interpreted as the predicate syllable-final?. Without clustering, selection of this factor would result in a three-way split.
Further examination of this tree suggests additional conditions on this
generalization. For example, the branch leading to node 2 specifies that
the following-dictionary-symbol should belong to a subset composed primarily of voiced sounds; in particular, all semivowels and nasals plus
some voiced fricatives and tense vowels are enumerated. In contrast, the

branch leading to node 1 specifies that the following-dictionary-symbol should belong to a subset composed primarily of plosives, unvoiced fricatives, and lax vowels. Additionally, the branches leading to nodes 3 and 4 specify a vocalic preceding-dictionary-symbol (E x R I W c o a r i l Y | e ∧ n N æ). A more precise rule can be defined which predicts that a /t/ in syllable-final position and preceded by a vocalic will be glottalized with greater likelihood when preceded by a vocalic in the branch leading to node 4 than a vocalic in the branch leading to node 3.

In Figure 5.4 is shown a context tree for predicting the phonetic elements of the dictionary symbol /y/. In this tree, the contextual factors of function-word? (fnc-word-p), foot-boundary-type (foot-bdry), and preceding-dictionary-symbol (prec-dict-sym) were selected for simultaneously differentiating among the phonetic elements of /y/. Four phonetic elements ([y],[ǰ] (jh), [š] (sh), and [ž] (zh)) plus deletion (−) were observed to occur. Terminal node 1 represents the prediction that when /y/ is in a function word and is preceded by either a /d/ or /č/, /y/ will be pronounced as [ǰ] 75% of the time and as [y] the remainder of the time.

5.3.6.1   Usefulness of additional contextual factors

The categories of contextual factor values formed by the clustering technique were examined. In particular, for each of the 45 dictionary symbols, a context tree was created. Each tree attempts to segregate all the variant pronunciations (phonetic elements) of a dictionary symbol based on the different contextual factors. The context trees were inspected to determine the categories formed from the values of the contextual factor preceding-dictionary-symbol and the values of the factor following-dictionary-symbol. At the root node of the tree, each factor has the set of 45 dictionary symbols plus a sentence-boundary marker as possible values. The sentence-boundary marker is used as the value of preceding-dictionary-symbol (following-dictionary-symbol) when the dictionary symbol corresponds to the initial (final) symbol representing a word in sentence-initial (sentence-final) position. As a tree is grown, the possible values at a node are dependent on contextual factors chosen closer to the root node. For instance, in Figure 5.4, foot-bdry is useful when prec-dict-sym is one of the values {h, v, f, k, m, b, g, n, l, p, z}.

We observed that many times the preceding and following context categories corresponded to linguistic categories, such as place or manner. For example, the next-dict-sym values in the tree predicting realizations of /s/ were clustered into the set {š, č, y} and the set of all other dictionary symbols. We also observed that the predominance

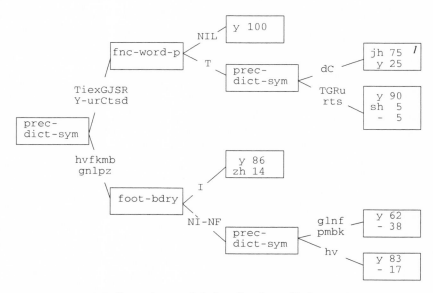

FIGURE 5.4 Pruned tree of /y/ realizations. Node numbers are
in the upper right corner of a box.

of **preceding-dictionary-symbol** and **following-dictionary-symbol** as useful
contextual factors was due in part to the flexibility in the possible ways of
grouping the factor values, since the number and components of groups
varied depending on the dictionary symbol and on the region of the tree,
or context, in which the clustering was done. Examination of contexts
near the terminal nodes of the trees were generally more understandable
since fewer phonetic elements typically were differentiated.

Triphone models, in which the preceding and following phone serve
as the context, have been the most popular type of contextual phone
model employed in speech recognition systems. To test the assumption
that **preceding-dictionary-symbol** and **following-dictionary-symbol** are the
most useful contextual factors, as in triphone models, the automatically-
selected contexts in the set of 45 context trees were examined. Twenty
of the trees ($p\ t\ k\ b\ d\ g\ m\ n\ w\ h\ u\ U\ i\ |\ I\ E\ x\ c\ s\ T$) had **preceding-
dictionary-symbol** and **following-dictionary-symbol** as their initial contexts
for splitting the data; in nine trees ($C\ J\ r\ l\ y\ e \wedge Z\ D$) **preceding-dictionary-
symbol** but not **following-dictionary-symbol** appeared in the first two levels; and in eight trees ($G\ o\ Y\ æ\ a\ z\ f\ v$) **following-dictionary-symbol** but
not **preceding-dictionary-symbol** appeared in the first two levels. This
agrees with the common working assumption that **preceding-dictionary-**

TABLE 5.5
Additional Contextual Factors
in Context Trees

Contextual Factor	Count
stress	13
function-word?	8
foot-boundary-type	5
syllable-boundary-type	5
syllable-part	3
open-syllable?	1
word-boundary-type	1

symbol and following-dictionary-symbol are the most important contexts for describing phonological variation. However, we also observed that other contexts are useful for differentiating among the realization distributions. The additional contextual factors which appeared in the first two levels of the tree and the number of times each appeared are shown in Table 5.5.

We also noted that for many of the trees in which the factors preceding-dictionary-symbol and following-dictionary-symbol were selected at the top two levels, other levels of the trees employed additional contextual factors. These observations indicate that the use of additional factors permits better modeling of phonological variation.

In summary, the preceding-dictionary-symbol and following-dictionary-symbol are the most generally useful contextual factors for predicting the variant pronunciations of the dictionary symbols. However, use of contextual factors other than, or in addition to, the preceding-dictionary-symbol and following-dictionary-symbol can provide better estimates of the likelihood of different realizations for individual dictionary symbols. We thus suggest the use of a mixed context unit based on the partitioning represented by the computed trees. That is, rather than using a fixed, consistent set of contextual factors, the mixed context units represented by tracing a path from the root node to each terminal node of a tree should be used. With this representation, the context of the phonetic elements of each terminal node are described only by the set of contextual factors encountered along the path.

The organization of the phonetic realizations into trees provides a way to specify contexts for creating models which are intermediate in the continuum from adjacent phone to whole-word models. In tree induction, a subset of factors which are good at differentiating among the phonetic element distributions is selected from a predetermined set. This subset is a larger number of contexts than the data would permit if the selected contexts were always considered together. Consequently, a larger overall number of contexts are used for describing the realizations. For example, in Figure 5.4, the three contexts of `prec-dict-sym`, `fnc-word-p`, and `foot-bdry` are used for describing the realizations of /y/, but only two contexts, either `prec-dict-sym` and `fnc-word-p` or `prec-dict-sym` and `foot-bdry`, are used to describe each terminal node. Furthermore, the effective number of contexts used to describe the conditions under which the different variants of a dictionary symbol occur is larger, given a limited amount of data.

5.3.6.2 Context tree properties

Context trees provide a contextual description composed of a subset of factors, as do production rules derived by hand. However, the rules encoded in context trees have several properties which make them amenable to creating pronunciation networks. A context tree partitions the space of contexts into mutually exclusive subspaces. This property simplifies checks on context compatibility when connecting networks. The tree structure, together with the data used to create a tree, also permits estimation of phonetic element distributions from either a full or partial context description. (Here we consider a context description to be partial if the context description does not match any terminal node in a context tree but does match at least one non-terminal. This can arise from missing factor values in the tree because the trees are data-derived.) Phonetic element distributions, in turn, can be used to predict how a dictionary symbol will be pronounced, as well as to reduce the size of a network systematically. In this section, these properties are described in more detail.

In a context tree, each pair of nodes in which neither node is a descendant of the other represents a pair of contexts which are mutually exclusive. Mutually exclusive contexts simplify the task of comparing and combining contexts in order to enforce the contextual constraints specified in a network modeling contextual effects. For example, with such a property, one can assume that once a matching constraint is found, one need not look any further.

The terminal nodes of a tree clearly represent mutually exclusive contexts. These nodes, together with the path leading to each node, can be interpreted as production rules for a set of mutually exclusive contexts. Then, given any context, the probability of each phonetic element occurring may be directly estimated from the counts encoded in a context tree because the contexts in the tree are mutually exclusive. In contrast, a set of hand-derived rules designed to describe a range of phonological phenomena will be unlikely to exhibit context descriptors that are mutually exclusive. Therefore, the probability of a phonetic element occurring in a particular context cannot be easily estimated.

Not all contexts will be guaranteed to be modeled in a context tree because the trees are dependent on the data from which they are derived. However, each node of a tree encodes the distribution of phonetic elements for the partial context represented by the node; consequently, phonetic element distributions in unobserved contexts may be estimated from a partial context specification by tracing down the tree until the observed value of a contextual factor no longer matches. Each phonetic realization of a dictionary symbol in a specified context translates into an arc in a network, and the phonetic element distributions can be encoded as arc transition probabilities. The probabilities provide a good initial estimate of the phonetic element distributions represented in the network and can be further refined by training the network when used in a hidden Markov model.

In a pronunciation network, the phonetic elements associated with a terminal node in a context tree are represented as a set of parallel arcs. A network may contain many instances of each "terminal node" since dictionary symbols and words may be repeated in different parts of the network. Each set of arcs that are derived from the same node should be constrained to have the same distribution. This can be accomplished in hidden Markov modeling by *tying* the probabilities across the instances of a phonetic element in a terminal node, that is, by constraining the probabilities to remain equal, as the pronunciation network is created and trained (Jelinek and Mercer 1980).

Information on phonetic element counts and distributions in context trees can be used to systematically reduce the size of pronunciation networks. The optimum number of pronunciations to use is unclear: with only a few pronunciations, recognition performance may not be optimal because acoustically distinct pronunciations of words are combined into one model; but with many pronunciations, recognizer performance may be poor because the amount of training data is sparse and unlikely pronunciations require additional computation to process. This is the problem described as "many additional parameters that need to be estimated with the same amount of training data" (Weintraub *et al.* 1989, p. 700). Weintraub and colleagues used measures of coverage and overgeneration of pronunciations to evaluate the networks created from their hand-derived phonological rules. Based on these measures, the set of phonological rules were then modified.

With context trees, the number of rules can be adjusted at the phonetic level. Using the phonetic element counts and distributions, unlikely phonetic elements can be removed from a terminal node to reduce the number of pronunciations. Pruning may be based upon counts of a phonetic element in a terminal node or upon the percentage of tokens of a phonetic element in a terminal node. In the first case, phonetic elements are removed when only a few tokens are observed. In the second case, unlikely phonetic elements are removed. In addition to reducing the number of pronunciations, pruning may also result in more robust predictions. For example, some of the infrequent phonetic element labels may be due to transcription error, and it would be judicious to remove them.

We have discussed some of the properties of context trees which make them suitable as a basis for creating pronunciation networks for which a richer set of contextual factors are incorporated. In the next section, we will describe how the trees are used to create pronunciation networks.

5.4   Pronunciation networks

This section describes a systematic method for creating pronunciation networks in which a wide variety of contextual factors are considered. The factors are selected through the use of the context trees, which contain information on possible pronunciations as well as estimates of the probabilities associated with each pronunciation. A phonetic level representation which can capture the predominant contextual effects is used.

A simple set of pronunciations for use in a speech recognition system can be obtained from a dictionary. However, dictionary pronunciations of words are relatively coarse-grained. Speech recognition systems that represent words with sub-word units generally use phonetic elements rather than dictionary baseforms because the pronunciations of a dictionary symbol may be very different, as measured by the acoustic similarity metrics commonly employed in recognition systems. The phonetically-based pronunciations are usually represented compactly in a pronunciation network. In this section, we describe the automatic creation of phonetically-based pronunciation networks from dictionary baseforms. Such a procedure enables one to add new words to a lexicon of pronunciations, in which the lookup is dictionary-based and a network modeling pronunciation variation is automatically created.

5.4.1   From tree to network

Pronunciation networks can be created from context trees by mapping the dictionary pronunciation of a word into a phonetic representation specified by the context trees. The terminal nodes of the context trees serve as the "alphabet" for creating word networks. Each terminal node represents a one-to-many mapping between a dictionary symbol in a particular context and a set of phonetic elements, with possible adjacent contextual constraints which limit the phonetic elements that can be joined.

The mapping from a dictionary baseform to a set of possible pronunciations is characterized by the substitution, deletion, and insertion of phonetic elements. Each dictionary symbol may be realized as a phonetic element or it may be deleted. Therefore, substitution and deletion of a dictionary symbol are treated identically when mapping a dictionary baseform into a network of phonetic elements. The 45 context trees, discussed in Section 5.3.6.1, are used to describe the observed substitutions and deletions of each of the dictionary symbols in transcriptions of speech. One context tree is created for each of the dictionary symbols and the data in a tree defines the set of phonetic elements observed in each context. For compatibility, the same dictionary used to create the context trees, the *X-Dictionary*, is used for network creation.

5.4.2 Modeling insertions

In addition to modeling substitutions and deletions, as the context trees do, pronunciation network creation also requires modeling of insertions. Insertions do not fit the substitution/deletion model in which a dictionary symbol is realized as a phonetic element. Instead, insertions may occur *between* any pair of dictionary symbols and are characterized by the context of dictionary symbols *adjacent* to the location of a possible insertion. Contextual factors are redefined by replacing each factor describing a dictionary symbol with contextual factors describing adjacent dictionary symbols. For example, the factor stress is replaced with stress-of-preceding-dictionary-symbol and stress-of-following-dictionary-symbol.

By modeling when insertions do *not* occur, the probability of an insertion in any context can be predicted. These requirements are met by representing all insertions and non-insertions in one tree, an *insertion tree*, in which the contextual factors are redefined to be a set applicable to insertions. In organizing the data to build an insertion tree, all pairs of dictionary symbols in the training data are checked for whether or not an insertion occurred between them. If so, the context and type of insertion is noted; if not, the context and the fact that no insertion occurred is noted. The insertion tree thus predicts when insertions can occur, as well as what type of insertion can occur in a particular context.

5.4.3 Selection of adjacent contexts

In the creation of a pronunciation network, the selection of which preceding and following contexts to use must be considered with care. Although it is possible to create context trees with a two-level representation in which the preceding and following dictionary symbol and preceding and following phonetic elements are included as contextual factors[4], including both the preceding and following phonetic elements as contextual factors in pronunciation network creation results in an unsatisfiable condition: a network cannot be built sequentially from either the left or right if more than one of the contexts of preceding phonetic element or following phonetic element is used as a conditioning context.

Expressing this more formally, the dictionary pronunciation of a word is represented as a sequence of N dictionary symbols, $\{x_1, x_2, \ldots, x_N\}$. The *lexical* context of each dictionary symbol, x_i, is described by a vector $\mathbf{l}_i$ which is composed of the values of the lexical contextual factors of x_i; that is, the values dependent upon phonetic element information are not included. Between each pair of dictionary symbols an insertion may occur. The context of a possible insertion is described by a vector $\mathbf{b}_j (j = 1, \ldots, N - 1)$ composed of the values of the lexically-based contextual factors relevant to an insertion. The sequence of contextual factor values describing the sequence of dictionary symbols is of length $2N - 1$ and is composed of a vector describing the lexical factor values of a dictionary symbol alternating with a vector describing the insertion factor values. The sequence may be expressed as: $\mathbf{C} = \{\mathbf{l}_1, \mathbf{b}_1, \mathbf{l}_2, \mathbf{b}_2, \ldots, \mathbf{b}_{N-1}, \mathbf{l}_N\} = \{\mathbf{c}_1, \mathbf{c}_2, \ldots, \mathbf{c}_{2N-1}\}$.

For ease of notation, the value of a phonetic element label is *nil* when a deletion occurs or an insertion does not occur. Then the desired output phonetic element sequence, which contains substitutions, deletions, and insertions, may be expressed as: $\mathbf{y} = \{y_1, y_2, \ldots, y_{2N-1}\}$. Note that the number of non-nil phonetic elements need not be equal to the number of dictionary symbols, N, due to insertions and deletions. Using Bayes' theorem, the probability of a phonetic element sequence, when given a particular lexical context sequence, $\mathbf{C}$, can be represented as:

(1) $\quad Pr(y_1, y_2, \ldots, y_{2N-1}|\mathbf{C}) =$
$Pr(y_1|y_2, \ldots, y_{2N-1}, \mathbf{C})Pr(y_2|y_3, \ldots, y_{2N-1}, \mathbf{C}) \ldots Pr(y_{2N-1}|\mathbf{C})$.

If we assume that the farthest phonetic elements to influence the realization of a dictionary symbol are adjacent phonetic elements, then equation (1) can be rewritten as:

(2) $\quad Pr(y_1, y_2, \ldots, y_{2N-1}|\mathbf{C}) =$
$Pr(y_1|y_2, \mathbf{C})Pr(y_2|y_3, \mathbf{C}) \ldots Pr(y_{2N-1}|\mathbf{C})$

when the phonetic element is conditioned on the following phonetic el-

---

[4]A related idea, two-level morphology, is described in Koskenniemi (1983a,b) and Karttunen (1983).

ement only. Similarly, the output can be conditioned on the preceding
phonetic element only:

(3) $Pr(y_1, y_2, \ldots, y_{2N-1}|\mathbf{C}) =$
      $Pr(y_{2N-1}|y_{2N-2}, \mathbf{C})Pr(y_{2N-2}|y_{2N-3}, \mathbf{C}) \ldots Pr(y_1|\mathbf{C}).$

From equations (2) and (3) we see that the conditioning cannot be on
both the preceding phonetic element and following phonetic element simultaneously. Let p_i and f_i represent the value of the contextual factors
preceding-phonetic-element and following-phonetic-element, respectively,
for dictionary symbol i. Thus the allowable sets of contextual factors
for describing the mapping from dictionary symbol x_i to phonetic ele-
ment y_i when building a pronunciation network are $\{\mathbf{C}, p_i\}$, $\{\mathbf{C}, f_i\}$,
and $\{\mathbf{C}\}$. In the last case, the information provided at the phonetic level
is ignored. If we also assume that adjacent dictionary symbols are the
furthest dictionary symbols that influence the realization of a dictionary
symbol or insertion, equation (2) can be rewritten as:

$$Pr(y_1, y_2, \ldots, y_{2N-1}|\mathbf{C}) =$$
$$Pr(y_1|y_2, \mathbf{c}_1, \mathbf{c}_2)Pr(y_2|y_3, \mathbf{c}_1, \mathbf{c}_2, \mathbf{c}_3) \ldots Pr(y_{2N-1}|\mathbf{c}_{2N-2}, \mathbf{c}_{2N-1}).$$

In our experiments, the contextual factors preceding-phonetic-element
and following-phonetic-element did not occur in the 45 pruned *context*
trees, so the pronunciation networks that we describe are derived without
conditioning on either the preceding or following phonetic element. However, the contextual factors preceding-phonetic-element and following-
phonetic-element were both observed in the *insertion* tree. Although
both phonetic element contexts cannot be accommodated in a one pass
process, as we have just seen, both phonetic element contexts in the insertion tree can be accommodated by creating the network in a two pass
process. In the first pass, dictionary symbols are mapped to phonetic elements, accounting for substitutions and deletions only. The context of
the dictionary symbol sequence is described by the lexical context only:
$\mathbf{L} = \{l_1, l_2, \ldots, l_N\}$. In the second pass, the phonetic elements needed to
describe the context of each possible insertion point are now known, so
an insertion tree containing phonetic element-based contextual factors
can be used to add insertions.

5.4.4   Network creation

Networks are created word by word and can be joined to produce a pronunciation network for a recognition system. Networks created using adjacent contexts, such as preceding and following dictionary symbol and
preceding or following phonetic element, explicitly model cross-word-
boundary contextual effects. If the context at the word boundaries is
unknown, as when the word network is to be connected to a variety

of contexts, the phonetic elements occurring in each context and corresponding probabilities are enumerated. With this method, one network can be created for each word, and a network modeling sentences can be created later from the word networks. Alternatively, if the adjacent words are known, the phonetic elements at the word boundary are known, and only these phonetic elements need to be listed. With the latter method, word-boundary dictionary symbols can be treated the same as word-internal dictionary symbols.

In the previous section, it was shown that at most one phonetic element context may be used when modeling substitutions and deletions, but by using a two-pass process, a word network in which the context of an insertion is described by adjacent phonetic element values could be created. In particular, the context of each dictionary symbol in a word is matched to the appropriate context tree. The context of a node in a context tree is described by the contextual factor values encountered in traversing the tree from the root node to that node. For each dictionary symbol, the associated phonetic element distribution at the best matching node (usually a terminal node) in the tree is represented as a set of parallel arcs, one arc per phonetic element. This produces a sequence of parallel arcs representing phonetic elements, which in turn, represent the sequence of dictionary symbols. If either the preceding or following phonetic element is considered, then the mapping is done either from left to right or right to left, respectively. Contextual constraints associated with the phonetic elements at a context tree node are matched to contextual constraints of the adjacent arcs.

After each dictionary symbol is replaced by arcs representing substitutions and deletions, the phonetic context of each possible insertion is revealed. A check for possible insertions based on the current context and the insertion tree is performed and insertions are added between the arcs when the context for an insertion is compatible. If a phonetic context was to be considered, then the network would be created from the left or the right, depending on whether the preceding or following phonetic element was employed.

Using our method based on context trees, the creation of a pronunciation network for the word 'fence' is shown in Figure 5.5. In Figure 5.5a, the phonetic elements representing each dictionary symbol are shown as labeled arcs. In the given context, the dictionary symbol /n/ is represented as two phonetic elements, [n] and [en], with [n] occurring 94% of the time. The contextual factors describing adjacent phonetic elements for modeling substitutions and deletions were not considered in creating this network. Each set of arcs from a node are connected to produce the simple network in Figure 5.5b. Addition of insertions, in which we

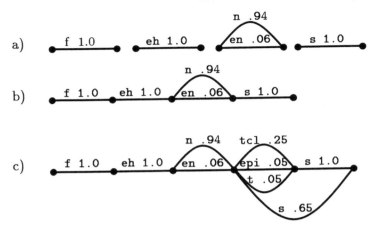

FIGURE 5.5 Pronunciation network for 'fence': (a) initial arcs
(b) arcs connected (c) insertions added. Phonetic element
symbols are defined in Table 2.1 and Table 2.2.

do include the contextual factors describing adjacent phonetic elements
produces the network shown in Figure 5.5c. Here a t-closure, (tcl), is
the most likely insertion. Other possible insertions at this point are an
epenthetic closure, (epi), and a t-release, (t).

In creating this network, the word was assumed to be spoken in
isolation and therefore was preceded and followed by silence. Had a
context not been specified, the boundaries of the word would be more
bushy with additional arcs representing the different possible phonetic
elements and probabilities in various contexts. For example, an /s/ in
word-final position is more likely to be palatalized and pronounced as
an [š] when followed by a /y/ or an /š/, as in 'fence your' or 'fence
should', than when followed by a vowel, as in 'fence any'. When the
context of a word is not specified, possible palatalization of the word-
final /s/ is modeled by replacing each [s] arc with three parallel arcs.
One arc is assigned a contextual constraint prohibiting any following
dictionary symbol for which a correspondence with palatalization has
been observed in the data. This arc represents the [s] phonetic element
with a probability of 1.0 since [s] is the only phonetic element which
was observed to occur in the given context. The other two arcs are
assigned the contextual constraint that the following dictionary symbol
is required to be one for which /s/ palatalization has been observed to
occur. One arc represents the [s] phonetic element and the other arc
represents the [š] phonetic element; the probabilities of the two arcs
sum to 1.0. This models the observation that when /s/ is followed by a

dictionary symbol for which palatalization occurs, /s/ is palatalized only some of the time. A flapped /t/ is another example of the likelihood of the occurrence of a phonetic element being dependent upon context: in word-final position it is more likely to occur if followed by an unstressed vowel, as in 'ate a', than when followed by a nasal, as in 'ate no'.

When the context of a word is unknown and all word boundary contexts must be listed, unobserved cross-word-boundary contexts may be handled by including a set of *default arcs*. The distribution of all observed phonetic elements across all contexts (the distribution at the root node) is represented using one default arc per phonetic element. Default arcs are also used when the context of a dictionary baseform does not match any context represented by the other arcs. A more detailed estimate of the phonetic element distribution could be made by using an ordered set of default arcs representing the distribution of observed phonetic elements in the non-terminal nodes of the tree. The default arcs are ordered such that the arcs corresponding to the node with the most matching factors are used. By using default arcs, a pronunciation network can be created for any word from a dictionary baseform.

5.5 Conclusions

In this chapter, we have advocated a phonetically-based representation with an enriched set of contextual descriptors for providing a general framework in which new words may be easily added to the vocabulary. A wide variety of factors is used to model contextual effects, including long-range and cross-word boundary phenomena.

We presented a systematic, data-intensive approach for describing and modeling phonological variation. By basing the models on a large data set, counts of the occurrence of different variants are available for producing robust models. However, these models are only as good as the data. As with other statistical techniques, even with a "large" amount of data, the models are not the "best" models, though they are "good" models.

The contexts identified are derived from the phonological variation exhibited in a large hand-transcribed database of utterances. The distribution of phonetic elements will vary from speaker to speaker due to speaker characteristics and dialect differences. The database we used, TIMIT, was designed to sample speech from many speakers. If instead, the speech from one speaker is represented in the data, then a pronunciation tailored to that speaker will be created.

The combination of decision tree induction and agglomerative clustering organizes the realization data into a representation conditioned on context. The tree induction attempts to separate different phonetic elements, while the agglomerative clustering provides for grouping of the context values into a small number of categories, which can often be related to linguistic categories. The smaller number of categories allows for better estimates of the realization distributions, and the use of a tree structure allows multiple mutually exclusive context sets to be used to describe phonetic element distributions. The trees can be traversed to produce pronunciation distributions for each symbol in a dictionary baseform. A mixed context description, as specified by the terminal nodes of the context trees, rather than the set of contexts in the trees, was advocated for building pronunciation networks for speech recognition systems. This permits the large number of dimensions entailed by a greater number of contextual descriptors for predicting pronunciation variation to be handled. Context trees were shown to possess properties, such as the ability to estimate distributions from partial contexts and the capacity to systematically reduce the size of a network based on the tree data, that make the trees a good representation from which to create pronunciation networks. From the set of context trees, one per dictionary symbol, plus an insertion tree, pronunciation networks can be automatically created to represent the alternative pronunciations of a dictionary baseform.

6

Final remarks

In this monograph, we have discussed several methods of modeling phonological variation which draw on the fields of linguistics, statistics, and engineering. We now conclude with several observations regarding modeling the way people speak and regarding the transfer of basic research to the domain of speech technology.

In these chapters, we made no attempt to develop a complete, causal account of American speech. Such an enterprise would presumably encompass factors ranging from mood to social circumstance to articulatory motor control. We did show that it is possible to model transcribed data of a cross-section of the population without appeal to hand-ordered rules, if overgeneration of pronunciations is constrained through the use of contextual descriptors including boundary information, prosodic units, and stress. This laid the groundwork for a closer investigation of such contextual descriptors and for the development of a methodology for automatically creating probabilistic word models.

Developing such a methodology for speech recognition, or in general, transferring theoretical advances to the domain of engineering practice, is a demanding task. One general problem is the interpretation, or correct application, of fundamental results. In the application of linguistic theory to speech technology, it is not enough to prove, say, that prosodic units figure in the description of certain crucial phenomena in the world's languages—when to use which prosodic descriptors emerges as a practical obstacle to surmount. Good coverage is a prerequisite to adequate signal-based technology. For instance, an observation may have been made that the preceding and following elements determine the acoustic properties of a certain sound. Someone wishing to apply this result needs information about the coverage of this finding, or else may interpret it as applicable to a wide range of data. A system may then be built which uses triphones to model *all* sounds. Such an interpretation of phonetic findings is benign for simple cases, but is not when more sophisticated analytical results of sound variation are considered.

We have developed one technique, the algorithm for computing context trees, which is intended to harness the power of abstract linguistic descriptors of speech. It represents a more general methodology for finding models given a set of observations and a variety of possibly competing theoretical descriptors. We have also shown how to use this methodology in the automatic creation of probabilistic pronunciation networks, the data structures that form the skeleton of current speech recognition systems. In the future, new data structures for representing spoken language may be developed, but we will still require techniques for evaluating contextual factors—be they physical, social, or simply resident in the linguistic knowledge of a speaker—against the data at hand in order to test our theoretical progress and make use of what we learn.

Appendix A

Coverage of the PPS

The following numbers show the result of the coverage experiment described in Chapters 3 and 4. The words given below are those produced by the readers of the 500 TIMIT sentences (along with their transcriptions) which were not produced by the generation system.

```
(test-coverage)
;; fusions-test

500 utterances,
4291 words,
213 new variants,
(99.95% correct)
```

'sudden' (sʌdn̩)	⇒	sʌʔn̩.
'blistered' (blɪstr̩d)	⇒	blɪsr̩d.
'A' ((e ə))	⇒	m̩.
'ended' (ɛndɨd)	⇒	ɛndɪd.
'stopwatch' (stapwɔč)	⇒	stapwatč.
'particularly' (pr̩tɪkyulr̩li)	⇒	pr̩tɪküli.
'sprained' (sprend)	⇒	spreŋ.
'Don't' (dont)	⇒	dʊn.
'but' (bʌt)	⇒	bɨt.
'prefers' (prifr̩z)	⇒	pr̩fr̩s.
'a' ((e ə))	⇒	NIL.
'anecdotal' (ænɛkdotl̩)	⇒	ænɨkdorl̩.
'Tofu' (tofu)	⇒	tufɨ.
'potatoes' (pətetoz)	⇒	pɨtedɨz.
'Shaving' (ševɨŋ)	⇒	ševiŋ.
'item' (aʸtm̩)	⇒	aʸɾɨm.
'remote' (rimot)	⇒	rr̩mot.
'government' ((gʌvr̩nmənt gʌvəmənt))	⇒	gʌvr̩mɛnt.

'regarding' (rigardɨŋ) ⇒ rigarɾɪŋ.
'maintenance' (mentɨnɨns) ⇒ meʔnɪnts.
'takes' (teks) ⇒ tekš.
'strong' (strɔŋ) ⇒ šrɔŋ.
'giant' (jaʸɨnt) ⇒ djaʸənʔ.
'glistening' (glɪsn̩ɨŋ) ⇒ glɪsnɪŋ.
'autographs' (ɔtɨgræfs) ⇒ ɔɾɡræfs.
'animals' (ænɨml̩z) ⇒ ænəml̩z.
'Amoebas' (əmibəz) ⇒ həmibʌz.
'change' (čenǰ) ⇒ tčendš.
'constantly' (kanstɨntli) ⇒ kanstəli.
'chosen' (čozn̩) ⇒ tčozən.
'straightforward' (stretfɔrwr̩d) ⇒ streʔfɔɾɾ.
'always' ((ɔlwez ɔlwiz)) ⇒ ɔwəz.
'Angora' (æŋgorə) ⇒ æŋgɔɾ.
'Nonprofit' (nanprafət) ⇒ nanprafɪʔ.

'seeking' (sikɨŋ) ⇒ sikiŋ.
'students" (studn̩ts) ⇒ stüʔn̩ts.
'notices' (notɨsəz) ⇒ noɾɨsɪz.
'suggestion' (səgǰɛsčn̩) ⇒ sɨgǰɛgštčɨn.
'bibliographies' (bɪbliagrəfiz) ⇒ bɪbliagr̩fiz.
'course' (kors) ⇒ kɔrš.
'Pizzerias' (pitsr̩iəz) ⇒ pitzr̩riəz.
'before' (bifor) ⇒ bəfɔr.
'fascinating' (fæsn̩etɨŋ) ⇒ fæsɨneɾiŋ.
'Children' (čɪldrən) ⇒ čɪlɾr̩n.
'good' (gʊd) ⇒ gʊdɨ.
'generous' (ǰenr̩ɨs) ⇒ djɛnɾʌs.
'entertaining' (ɛntr̩tenɨŋ) ⇒ ɨnr̩teniŋ.
'a' ((e ə)) ⇒ r̩.
'a' ((e ə)) ⇒ NɪL.
'obtaining' (əbtenɨŋ) ⇒ əbtenin.
'pleasantly' (plɛzn̩tli) ⇒ plɛzənʔli.
'miraculously' (mr̩ækyʊləsli) ⇒ mr̩ækyɨləsli.
'chablis' (šæbli) ⇒ šɨbli.
'While' (hwaʸl) ⇒ wl̩.
'waiting' (wetɨŋ) ⇒ weɾiŋ.

'before' (bifor) ⇒ bəfɔr.
'postponed' (postpond) ⇒ pospon.
'the' ((ðə ði)) ⇒ ðl̩.
'splinter' (splɪntr̩) ⇒ splɪndr̩.
'mercilessly' (mr̩sɨlɛsli) ⇒ mr̩sələsli.
'potatoes' (pətetoz) ⇒ pɪteɾoz.
'haven't' (hævn̩t) ⇒ hævənt.
'of' (əv) ⇒ v.
'a' ((e ə)) ⇒ ðə.
'education' (ɛjɨkešɨn) ⇒ ɨdjɨkešn̩.
'Agricultural' (ægrɪkʌlčr̩l̩) ⇒ ægr̩kʌltčr̩l̩.
'products' (pradʌkts) ⇒ praɾɨkts.
'rationalize' (ræšn̩laʸz) ⇒ ræšn̩laʸz.
'distance' (dɪstɨns) ⇒ dɪstɨnts.

'a' ((e ə))	⇒	ðə.
'of' (əv)	⇒	r̥v.
'bandaged' (bændɪjd)	⇒	bændidj.
'the' ((ðə ði))	⇒	NIL.
'repainting' (ripentɨŋ)	⇒	ripeniŋ.
'caused' (kczd)	⇒	kɔst.
'presented' (prizɛntɨd)	⇒	pr̥zɛnɨd.
'webbed' (wɛbd)	⇒	wɛbdɨ.
'vegetables' (vɛjtəbl̩z)	⇒	vɛdjtbl̩z.
'making' (mekɨŋ)	⇒	mekiŋg.
'modelling' (madɨlɨŋ)	⇒	mar̥lɨŋ.
'security' (sɨkyr̥ɨti)	⇒	sɨkr̥r̥i.
'resemble' (rɨzɛmbl̩)	⇒	rizɛmbl̩.
'aptitude' (æptɨtud)	⇒	æpttür̥.
'judged' (jʌjd)	⇒	djʌžd.
'by' (baʸ)	⇒	bʌ.
'intelligible' (ɪntɛləjɨbl̩)	⇒	ɪntɛlɨdjəbl̩.
'an' (æn)	⇒	ɨʔn.
'tastes' (tests)	⇒	test.
'frequently' (frikwəntli)	⇒	frikwʌnʔliy.
'Top' (tap)	⇒	tab.
'zinnias' (zɪniəz)	⇒	zenyɨz.
'crooked' (krʊkɨd)	⇒	kr̥kɨd.
'attendance' (ətɛndɨns)	⇒	tɛndɛns.
'seldom' (sɛldəm)	⇒	zɛldəm.
'required' (rikwaʸrd)	⇒	r̥kwaʸr̥d.
'Mosquitoes' (məskitoz)	⇒	məskiož.
'humid' (hyumɨd)	⇒	hyumɪd.
'appreciated' (əprišietɨd)	⇒	əpriʔšʔɪerɨd.
'into' (ɪntu)	⇒	ɨntʊ.
'gift' (gɪft)	⇒	kyɪft.
'had' (hæd)	⇒	hædj.
'Don't' (dont)	⇒	dor̥.
'like' (laʸk)	⇒	lik.
'Sequoia' (sɪkwoʸə)	⇒	sɨkoʸyɨ.
'general's' (jɛnr̥l̩z)	⇒	djɛnrɨlz.
'intelligence' (ɪntɛlɨjɨns)	⇒	ɨntɛlədjɛns.
'challenged' (čælɨnjd)	⇒	čælɛnžd.
'like' (laʸk)	⇒	lik.
'government' ((gʌvr̥nmənt gʌvəmənt))	⇒	gʌvm̩ɨnt.
'without' (wɪθǎʸt)	⇒	wəðǎʸt.
'in' (ɪn)	⇒	ɪn̩.
'experiment's' (ɛkspɛrəmənts)	⇒	kspɪrɨmɛnts.
'unexpected' (ʌnɛkspɛktɨd)	⇒	ʌnɨkspɛktɨd.
'How' (hǎʸ)	⇒	hǎʸw.
'escalator' (ɛskələtr̥)	⇒	ɛskyɨlɛr̥r̥.
'Hungarian' (hʌŋgɛriən)	⇒	həngɛriɨn.
'and' (ænd)	⇒	ɨŋ.
'uninterrupted' (ʌnɪntr̥ʌptɨd)	⇒	ʌnɨnɨrʌptɨd.
'others' (ʌðr̥z)	⇒	ʌðʊz.

'The' ((ðə ði))	⇒	di.
'didn't' ((dɪdɨnt dɪdṇt))	⇒	dɪʔṇ.
'wandered' (wandṛd)	⇒	wandɪd.
'with' (wɪθ)	⇒	wɪʔt.
'aggressive' (əgrɛsɨv)	⇒	ɪgrɛsɪv.
'policeman' (pəlismən)	⇒	plismɨn.
'barracuda' (bærəkudə)	⇒	bɛɾkürɽ.
'recoiled' (rikoʸld)	⇒	rikoʸld.
'zoologist' (zoaləjɨst)	⇒	züalədjɨs.
'relaxed' (rilækst)	⇒	rɨlæks.
'throughout' (θruáʸt)	⇒	θruot.
'ideal' (aʸdil)	⇒	aʸdiə.
'hours' (áʸrz)	⇒	áʸr̥z.
'hours' (áʸrz)	⇒	áʸr̥z.
'The' ((ðə ði))	⇒	ðɽ.
'sherbet' (šṛbɨt)	⇒	šṛbr̥t.
'shrapnel' (šræpnḷ)	⇒	šrapnɛl.
'in' (ɪn)	⇒	ṇ.
'oily' (oʸli)	⇒	oli.
'and' (ænd)	⇒	ɨm.
'mediocrity' (midiakrɨti)	⇒	miɾiokr̥ti.
'allow' (əláʸ)	⇒	ɨlo.
'didn't' ((dɪdɨnt dɪdṇt))	⇒	dɪʔṇ.
'cannot' ((kænnat kænnat))	⇒	kɨnat.
'algebraic' (æljɨbreɪk)	⇒	ældjṛbreɪk.
'conditions' (kəndɪšɨnz)	⇒	kɨndɪšṇz.
'Will' (wɪl)	⇒	wɪ.
'remained' (rimend)	⇒	rɨmen.
'pearls' (pṛlz)	⇒	pṛlz.
'eating' (itɨŋ)	⇒	iɾiŋ.
'you' (yu)	⇒	hyü.
'Cliff's' (klɪfs)	⇒	klɨfs.
'in' (ɪn)	⇒	ɪŋŋ.
'Remember' (rimɛmbṛ)	⇒	rimɛmṛ.
'splurged' (splṛjd)	⇒	zplṛjd.
'and' (ænd)	⇒	ṃ.
'Plymouth' (plɪməθ)	⇒	plɪmɨθ.
'greasy' ((grisi grizi))	⇒	grɪsi.
'auburn' (ɔbṛn)	⇒	arbṛn.
'choosing' (čuzɨŋ)	⇒	tčoʸzin.
'requires' (rikwaʸrz)	⇒	rəkwaʸr̥z.
'expertise' (ɛkspṛtiz)	⇒	ɛkšpr̥tiz.
'Thomas' (tamɨs)	⇒	taməs.
'problem' (prabləm)	⇒	prablm.
'haunted' (hɔntɨd)	⇒	hɔnɪd.
'was' (wəz)	⇒	wəð.
'audiovisual' (ɔdiovɪžuḷ)	⇒	ɔɾiɨvɪžwḷ.
'below' (bilo)	⇒	bḷow.
'was' (wəz)	⇒	wəð.
'Cooperation' (koapṛešṇ)	⇒	kwɔpṛešɨn.
'understanding' (ʌndṛstændɨŋ)	⇒	ṇdʌnṛstændɨŋ.

'triumphant' (tra^{y}ʌmfənt) ⇒ tra^{y}əmfənʔ.
'exhibited' (ɪgzɪbɨtɨd) ⇒ ɨgzɪbɨɨd.
'heroism' (hɛroɪzm̩) ⇒ hɛrozəm.
'forces' (fɔrsəz) ⇒ fɔsɨz.
'huge' (hyuǰ) ⇒ hüž.
'Suburban' (səbɹbɨn) ⇒ səbɹbɨɨn.
'housewives' (hǎ^{v}swa^{y}vz) ⇒ hǎ^{v}swa^{y}võ.
'gab' (gæb) ⇒ gæəb.
'tips' (tɪps) ⇒ tɪəps.
'cooking' (kʊkɨŋ) ⇒ kʊkiŋ.
'Primitive' (prɪmətɪv) ⇒ pɹmɨɾɨv.
'cooperates' (koapɹets) ⇒ koopɹets.
'dressing' (drɛsɨŋ) ⇒ drɛsiŋ.

'connoisseur' (kanɨsɹ̩) ⇒ kanʌsʊɹ.
'updating' (ʌpdetɨŋ) ⇒ ʌpdeɾiŋ.
'discouraging' (dɪskɹɨǰɨŋ) ⇒ ɨskɹɨdjiŋ.
'ointment' (o^{y}ntmənt) ⇒ o^{y}mɨnʔ.
'The' ((ðə ði)) ⇒ ðn̩.
'refurbishing' (rifɹbɨšɨŋ) ⇒ rifɹbɨšiŋ.
'bureaucracy' (byɹakrɨsi) ⇒ byɹakɹsi.
'audiovisual' (ɔdiovɪžuḷ) ⇒ ɔɾiovɪžwəl.
'appointed' (əpo^{y}ntɨd) ⇒ əpo^{y}nɨ.
'Cooperation' (koapɹešn̩) ⇒ koopɹešən.
'contributed' (kəntrɪbyutɨd) ⇒ kn̩trɪütɨd.
'complex' (kəmplɛks) ⇒ kamplɛks.
'yards' (yardz) ⇒ yaɹdz.
'colleges' (kalɪǰəz) ⇒ kalɪdjɪz.
'coeducational' (koɛǰukešṇḷ) ⇒ koɛdjɨkešṇḷ.
'available' (əvelɨbḷ) ⇒ əvɛləbḷ.
'the' ((ðə ði)) ⇒ ð.

'spurious' (spyʊriəs) ⇒ spɹiɨs.
'fjords' (fiɔrdz) ⇒ fyɔrdz.
'grow' (gro) ⇒ grow.
'so' (so) ⇒ sə.
'children' (čɪldrən) ⇒ tčɪldr̩n.
'using' (yuzɨŋ) ⇒ yüziŋ.
'antagonistic' (æntægənɪstɨk) ⇒ æntægɨnɪstɪk.
'jaguars' (ǰægwarz) ⇒ ǰægwaɹz.
'elm' (ɛlm) ⇒ ɨʔɛlm.
'disease' is not in the dictionary.
'provoked' (provokt) ⇒ pɹvokt.
'immediate' (ɪmidiət) ⇒ ɪnmiɾiɨt.
'Will' (wɪl) ⇒ wɨ.
'regarding' (rigardɨŋ) ⇒ rɨgarɾiŋ.

Appendix B

Cohorts produced by PPS

The following pages show the confusability cohorts produced by the generation system described in Chapters 3 and 4. The system produced a total of 68637 variants from 15343 words. There were 4.47 variants per word. The number of sets was 15343, with the average set size being 0.14, and the maximum set size 9. The percentage of unique items was 6.34.

Word: Set cardinality; Members.

a: [8] (is if ear it err ere air heir).
abate: [1] (obey).
accomplice: [1] (accomplish).
accomplish: [1] (accomplice).
Adam: [1] (atom).
add: [1] (at).
addition: [1] (edition).
admit: [2] (amid omit).
adorn: [1] (darn).
affect: [2] (fact effect).
affection: [1] (faction).
aid: [3] (ate aide eight).
aide: [3] (ate aid eight).
ail: [1] (ale).
ain't: [4] (and Ann an Anne).
air: [8] (a or her are heir err ere were).
aisle: [2] (I'll isle).
Al: [2] (all awl).
Alan: [1] (Allen).
ale: [1] (ail).
Ali: [1] (alley).
alight: [1] (elide).
all: [2] (Al awl).
Allen: [1] (Alan).
alley: [1] (Ali).

allow: [1] (lout).
altar: [1] (alter).
alter: [1] (altar).
amend: [1] (emend).
amid: [2] (admit omit).
among: [1] (monk).
an: [8] (end then one on in Ann ain't Anne).
and: [1] (ain't).
Ann: [6] (in end then an ain't Anne).
Anne: [6] (in end then Ann an ain't).
annex: [1] (next).
ant: [2] (end aunt).
anterior: [1] (interior).
appellate: [1] (pellet).
append: [1] (pent).
applaud: [1] (plod).
approximate: [1] (proximate).
arc: [1] (ark).
archer: [1] (orchard).
are: [9] (her heir err ere air were oar ore or).
ark: [1] (arc).
armor: [1] (army).
army: [1] (armor).
art: [1] (Art).
Art: [1] (art).
as: [3] (was is at).

ascend: [2] (ascent assent).
ascent: [2] (ascend assent).
aspire: [1] (espy).
ass: [1] (us).
assent: [2] (ascend ascent).
assume: [1] (soon).
assure: [4] (shirt share sir sure).
at: [3] (it add as).
ate: [3] (aide aid eight).
atom: [1] (Adam).
attain: [2] (tan taint).
auger: [1] (augur).
aught: [2] (ought odd).
augur: [1] (auger).
aunt: [2] (end ant).
awl: [2] (all Al).
aye: [2] (eye I).
bad: [1] (bat).
bade: [1] (bait).
bait: [1] (bade).
band: [1] (bang).
bandit: [1] (bandy).
bandy: [1] (bandit).
bang: [1] (band).
bar: [4] (boor Boer boar bore).
baron: [1] (barren).
barred: [1] (board).
barren: [1] (baron).
barrow: [2] (borough burrow).
bat: [1] (bad).
bawl: [1] (bought).
bazaar: [1] (bizarre).
be: [4] (bier beer bit bee).
beach: [1] (beech).
bead: [1] (beet).
bed: [1] (bet).
bee: [4] (bier beer bit be).
beech: [1] (beach).
been: [1] (bin).
beer: [4] (bee be bit bier).
beet: [1] (bead).
Belgian: [1] (Belgium).
Belgium: [1] (Belgian).
berry: [1] (bury).
Bert: [1] (bird).
berth: [1] (birth).
bet: [1] (bed).
better: [1] (Betty).
Betty: [1] (better).
bid: [1] (bit).
bidden: [2] (bitten bidding).
bidding: [1] (bidden).

bide: [3] (bite bight byte).
bier: [4] (bee be bit beer).
bight: [3] (bite bide byte).
bill: [1] (Bill).
Bill: [1] (bill).
bin: [1] (been).
bird: [1] (Bert).
birth: [1] (berth).
bit: [5] (bid bier beer bee be).
bite: [3] (bight bide byte).
bitten: [1] (bidden).
bizarre: [1] (bazaar).
bleat: [1] (bleed).
bleed: [1] (bleat).
bloc: [1] (block).
block: [1] (bloc).
boar: [4] (boor Boer bar bore).
board: [1] (barred).
boat: [1] (bode).
boatswain: [1] (bosun).
bode: [1] (boat).
Boer: [4] (boor boar bar bore).
bold: [1] (bolt).
bolt: [1] (bold).
bonnet: [1] (bonnie).
bonnie: [1] (bonnet).
boor: [4] (Boer boar bar bore).
boost: [1] (booze).
booze: [1] (boost).
bore: [4] (boor Boer boar bar).
borough: [2] (barrow burrow).
bosun: [1] (boatswain).
bought: [1] (bawl).
braise: [1] (braze).
brass: [1] (breast).
brat: [2] (bread bred).
brawl: [1] (brought).
braze: [1] (braise).
breach: [1] (breech).
bread: [2] (brat bred).
breast: [1] (brass).
bred: [2] (brat bread).
breech: [1] (breach).
bride: [1] (bright).
bright: [1] (bride).
Britain: [1] (Briton).
Briton: [1] (Britain).
broach: [1] (brooch).
broad: [1] (brought).
brooch: [1] (broach).
brood: [1] (brute).
brought: [2] (broad brawl).

brute: [1] (brood).
Bud: [3] (but bud butt).
bud: [3] (but Bud butt).
buffer: [1] (buffet).
buffet: [1] (buffer).
build: [1] (built).
built: [1] (build).
bullet: [1] (bully).
bully: [1] (bullet).
burrow: [2] (barrow borough).
bursa: [2] (bursar burst).
bursar: [1] (bursa).
burst: [1] (bursa).
bury: [1] (berry).
bus: [1] (buss).
buss: [1] (bus).
but: [3] (bud Bud butt).
butt: [3] (bud Bud but).
byte: [3] (bite bight bide).
cad: [1] (cat).
canape: [1] (canopy).
candor: [1] (candy).
candy: [1] (candor).
cannon: [1] (canon).
canon: [1] (cannon).
canopy: [1] (canape).
canter: [1] (cantor).
cantor: [1] (canter).
canvas: [1] (canvass).
canvass: [1] (canvas).
car: [5] (core cord chord corps cot).
carafe: [1] (craft).
carat: [3] (carrot caret karat).
caress: [2] (crass crest).
caret: [3] (carrot carat karat).
Carol: [1] (carol).
carol: [1] (Carol).
carriage: [1] (courage).
carrier: [1] (courier).
carrot: [3] (caret carat karat).
carry: [1] (curry).
cart: [3] (cord chord court).
cast: [1] (caste).
caste: [1] (cast).
cat: [1] (cad).
cause: [1] (cost).
cede: [2] (seed seat).
cent: [3] (send scent sent).
char: [2] (chore your).
chatter: [1] (chatty).
chatty: [1] (chatter).
chauffeur: [1] (sofa).

cheat: [1] (she).
check: [1] (Czech).
choir: [1] (quiet).
chord: [6] (cart court core car corps cord).
chore: [2] (char your).
chute: [1] (shoot).
cite: [3] (sight side site).
clammy: [1] (clamor).
clamor: [1] (clammy).
clod: [1] (clot).
clot: [1] (clod).
cloud: [1] (clout).
clout: [1] (cloud).
coarse: [1] (course).
coat: [3] (code corps core).
cod: [1] (cot).
code: [1] (coat).
coffee: [1] (coffer).
coffer: [1] (coffee).
cold: [1] (colt).
colonel: [1] (kernel).
colt: [1] (cold).
complement: [1] (compliment).
complementary: [1] (complimentary).
compliment: [1] (complement).
complimentary: [1] (complementary).
concede: [1] (conceit).
conceit: [1] (concede).
contend: [1] (content).
content: [1] (contend).
coolie: [1] (coolly).
coolly: [1] (coolie).
copper: [1] (copy).
copy: [1] (copper).
cord: [6] (cart court core car corps chord).
core: [5] (coat car cord chord corps).
corner: [1] (corny).
corny: [1] (corner).
corps: [5] (coat core car cord chord).
cost: [1] (cause).
cot: [2] (cod car).
council: [1] (counsel).
counsel: [1] (council).
counter: [1] (county).
county: [1] (counter).
courage: [1] (carriage).
courier: [1] (carrier).
course: [1] (coarse).
court: [3] (cart cord chord).
cover: [2] (covey covet).

covet: [1] (cover).
covey: [1] (cover).
craft: [1] (carafe).
crass: [2] (caress crest).
crest: [2] (crass caress).
cud: [1] (cut).
curd: [1] (curt).
currant: [1] (current).
current: [1] (currant).
curry: [1] (carry).
curt: [1] (curd).
cut: [1] (cud).
czar: [1] (tsar).
Czech: [1] (check).
dare: [3] (dirt do debt).
daring: [1] (during).
darn: [1] (adorn).
dead: [1] (debt).
dear: [2] (did deer).
debt: [3] (did dead dare).
deer: [2] (did dear).
depart: [1] (deport).
deport: [1] (depart).
descend: [2] (dissent descent).
descent: [2] (dissent descend).
did: [3] (debt deer dear).
dirt: [2] (dare do).
dissent: [2] (descent descend).
do: [2] (dirt dare).
does: [1] (dust).
doesn't: [1] (dozen).
dollar: [1] (dolly).
dolly: [1] (dollar).
done: [1] (dun).
dozen: [1] (doesn't).
draft: [1] (draught).
draught: [1] (draft).
dun: [1] (done).
during: [1] (daring).
dust: [1] (does).
ear: [4] (is if a it).
earn: [1] (urn).
ease: [1] (east).
east: [1] (ease).
eat: [3] (we he the).
eaten: [2] (eating Eden).
eating: [1] (eaten).
eddy: [1] (edit).
Eden: [1] (eaten).
edit: [1] (eddy).
edition: [1] (addition).
effect: [1] (affect).

eight: [3] (aide aid ate).
elide: [1] (alight).
elusive: [1] (illusive).
emend: [1] (amend).
end: [7] (aunt ant in Anne Ann
    an then).
enquire: [1] (inquire).
ere: [8] (a or her are heir err
    air were).
err: [8] (a or her are heir ere
    air were).
espy: [1] (aspire).
extend: [1] (extent).
extent: [1] (extend).
eye: [2] (aye I).
facile: [1] (vessel).
fact: [1] (affect).
faction: [1] (affection).
factor: [1] (vector).
fad: [1] (fat).
fade: [2] (fate fete).
fag: [1] (vague).
faint: [1] (feint).
fair: [1] (fare).
fairy: [1] (furry).
far: [3] (fore for four).
farce: [1] (force).
fare: [1] (fair).
farrow: [1] (furrow).
fast: [1] (vest).
fat: [3] (fed vet fad).
fate: [2] (fade fete).
fawn: [2] (fond font).
fear: [2] (fit fee).
feat: [2] (feet feed).
fed: [2] (fat vet).
fee: [2] (fit fear).
feed: [2] (feet feat).
feet: [2] (feat feed).
feint: [1] (faint).
felt: [1] (veldt).
fend: [1] (vent).
ferry: [1] (very).
fete: [2] (fade fate).
fever: [1] (viva).
file: [1] (viol).
filler: [2] (filly villa).
filly: [1] (filler).
fin: [2] (Finn vim).
finish: [1] (Finnish).
Finn: [2] (fin vim).
Finnish: [1] (finish).

fir: [1] (fur).
fire: [1] (vier).
first: [1] (verse).
fist: [1] (fizz).
fit: [2] (fear fee).
fizz: [1] (fist).
flair: [2] (flirt flare).
flare: [2] (flirt flair).
flat: [1] (fled).
flea: [2] (flit flee).
fled: [1] (flat).
flee: [2] (flit flea).
fling: [1] (flint).
flint: [1] (fling).
flirt: [2] (flare flair).
flit: [2] (flee flea).
flour: [1] (flout).
flout: [1] (flour).
foist: [1] (voice).
fold: [2] (volt vole).
fond: [2] (fawn font).
font: [2] (fond fawn).
for: [3] (fore far four).
force: [1] (farce).
fore: [3] (for far four).
fort: [1] (forte).
forte: [1] (fort).
forth: [1] (fourth).
found: [1] (fount).
fount: [1] (found).
four: [3] (fore for far).
fourth: [1] (forth).
franc: [1] (frank).
frank: [1] (franc).
freeze: [1] (frieze).
friar: [1] (fryer).
frieze: [1] (freeze).
from: [1] (fun).
fryer: [1] (friar).
fun: [1] (from).
fur: [1] (fir).
furnace: [1] (furnish).
furnish: [1] (furnace).
furrow: [1] (farrow).
furry: [1] (fairy).
gamin: [1] (gammon).
gammon: [1] (gamin).
had: [3] (hat has have).
hair: [1] (hare).
hairy: [2] (hurry harry).
hand: [1] (hang).
handsome: [1] (hansom).

hang: [1] (hand).
hansom: [1] (handsome).
hard: [4] (hoard horde hart heart).
hardy: [1] (hearty).
hare: [1] (hair).
harm: [1] (horn).
harry: [2] (hurry hairy).
hart: [2] (hard heart).
has: [4] (his hat had have).
haste: [1] (haze).
hat: [4] (head has had have).
have: [3] (hat has had).
haze: [1] (haste).
he: [7] (we eat the his here hear hit).
head: [1] (hat).
hear: [4] (his he hit here).
heard: [2] (herd hurt).
heart: [2] (hart hard).
hearty: [1] (hardy).
heat: [1] (heed).
heed: [1] (heat).
heir: [8] (a or her are err ere air
    were).
hen: [1] (hint).
her: [7] (or are heir err ere air
    were).
herd: [2] (heard hurt).
here: [4] (his he hit hear).
heron: [1] (herring).
herring: [1] (heron).
hid: [1] (hit).
him: [2] (inn in).
hint: [1] (hen).
his: [5] (here hear he hit has).
hit: [5] (hid his here hear he).
hoard: [2] (hard horde).
holy: [1] (wholly).
horde: [2] (hoard hard).
horn: [1] (harm).
hose: [1] (host).
host: [1] (hose).
hostel: [1] (hostile).
hostile: [1] (hostel).
hour: [3] (our how out).
how: [4] (our hour out hut).
hung: [1] (hunt).
hunt: [1] (hung).
hurdle: [1] (hurtle).
hurry: [2] (harry hairy).
hurt: [2] (herd heard).
hurtle: [1] (hurdle).
hut: [1] (how).

I: [2] (eye aye).
I'll: [2] (aisle isle).
id: [1] (it).
idle: [2] (idol idyl).
idol: [2] (idle idyl).
idyl: [2] (idol idle).
if: [6] (is ear a it of off).
illusive: [1] (elusive).
impart: [1] (import).
import: [1] (impart).
in: [8] (inn him end Anne Ann
then on an).
inflection: [1] (inflexion).
inflexion: [1] (inflection).
inn: [2] (in him).
inquire: [1] (enquire).
intend: [1] (intent).
intent: [1] (intend).
interior: [1] (anterior).
iris: [1] (Irish).
Irish: [1] (iris).
is: [7] (this if ear a it was as).
isle: [2] (I'll aisle).
it: [6] (id is if ear a at).
jam: [1] (jamb).
jamb: [1] (jam).
jar: [2] (jot your).
Jewry: [2] (juror jury).
jot: [1] (jar).
juror: [2] (jury Jewry).
jury: [2] (juror Jewry).
karat: [3] (carrot caret carat).
kennel: [1] (kindle).
kernel: [1] (colonel).
key: [2] (quay kit).
kid: [1] (kit).
kindle: [1] (kennel).
kit: [3] (kid quay key).
knave: [1] (nave).
knead: [2] (need neat).
knee: [3] (near knit no).
knew: [1] (new).
knight: [1] (night).
knit: [3] (near knee no).
knot: [2] (nod not).
know: [1] (no).
lackey: [1] (lacquer).
lacquer: [1] (lackey).
ladder: [3] (letter latter laddie).
laddie: [1] (ladder).
lag: [1] (leg).
laid: [1] (late).

lair: [1] (let).
lance: [1] (lens).
lancer: [1] (lancet).
lancet: [1] (lancer).
laser: [1] (lazy).
late: [1] (laid).
latter: [1] (ladder).
laud: [1] (lot).
laugh: [1] (left).
lazy: [1] (laser).
lea: [3] (leer lit lee).
lead: [2] (led let).
lean: [1] (lien).
led: [2] (lead let).
lee: [3] (leer lit leah).
leer: [3] (lee lea lit).
leery: [1] (lira).
left: [1] (laugh).
leg: [1] (lag).
lemming: [1] (lemon).
lemon: [1] (lemming).
lend: [1] (lent).
lens: [1] (lance).
lent: [1] (lend).
lessen: [1] (lesson).
lesson: [1] (lessen).
let: [3] (led lead lair).
letter: [1] (ladder).
levee: [2] (lever levy).
lever: [2] (levy levee).
levy: [2] (lever levee).
lewd: [2] (loot lute).
lichen: [2] (liken liking).
lid: [1] (lit).
lieder: [1] (litre).
lien: [1] (lean).
lift: [1] (live).
liken: [2] (lichen liking).
liking: [2] (liken lichen).
ling: [1] (lint).
lint: [1] (ling).
lion: [1] (lying).
lira: [1] (leery).
lit: [4] (lid leer lee leah).
litre: [1] (lieder).
live: [1] (lift).
load: [1] (lode).
loch: [1] (lock).
lock: [1] (loch).
locker: [1] (locket).
locket: [1] (locker).
lode: [1] (load).

loot: [2] (lewd lute).
lord: [1] (lore).
lore: [1] (lord).
lot: [1] (laud).
loud: [1] (lout).
lout: [2] (loud allow).
lustre: [1] (lusty).
lusty: [1] (lustre).
lute: [2] (loot lewd).
lying: [1] (lion).
mad: [1] (mat).
madder: [1] (matter).
made: [2] (maid mate).
maid: [2] (made mate).
main: [1] (mane).
mane: [1] (main).
manger: [1] (mangy).
mangy: [1] (manger).
manner: [1] (manor).
manor: [1] (manner).
mantel: [1] (mantle).
mantle: [1] (mantel).
mar: [2] (moor more).
mare: [1] (met).
marquess: [1] (marquis).
marquis: [1] (marquess).
marten: [1] (martin).
martin: [1] (marten).
mask: [1] (masque).
masque: [1] (mask).
mast: [1] (must).
mat: [1] (mad).
mate: [2] (maid made).
matter: [1] (madder).
may: [3] (mere me mitt).
me: [3] (mere may mitt).
mead: [3] (meet meat mete).
mean: [1] (mien).
meat: [3] (meet mead mete).
meddle: [1] (mettle).
meddler: [1] (medley).
medley: [1] (meddler).
meet: [3] (meat mead mete).
meld: [1] (melt).
melt: [1] (meld).
men: [1] (mint).
mend: [1] (mint).
mercer: [1] (mercy).
mercy: [1] (mercer).
mere: [3] (me may mitt).
merit: [1] (merry).
merry: [1] (merit).

met: [1] (mare).
mete: [3] (meet meat mead).
mettle: [1] (meddle).
mews: [1] (muse).
mid: [1] (mitt).
mien: [1] (mean).
might: [1] (mite).
mighty: [1] (mitre).
mil: [1] (mill).
miner: [1] (minor).
minor: [1] (miner).
mint: [2] (mend men).
mister: [1] (misty).
misty: [1] (mister).
mite: [1] (might).
mitre: [1] (mighty).
mitt: [4] (mid mere me may).
moat: [2] (mode mote).
mode: [2] (mote moat).
molar: [1] (moly).
mold: [1] (molt).
molder: [1] (motor).
molt: [1] (mold).
moly: [1] (molar).
monk: [1] (among).
moo: [1] (moue).
mood: [1] (moot).
moor: [2] (mar more).
moose: [1] (mousse).
moot: [1] (mood).
more: [2] (moor mar).
mote: [2] (mode moat).
motor: [1] (molder).
moue: [1] (moo).
mound: [1] (mount).
mount: [1] (mound).
mousse: [1] (moose).
mover: [1] (movie).
movie: [1] (mover).
mud: [1] (mutt).
mummer: [1] (mummy).
mummy: [1] (mummer).
muscle: [1] (mussel).
muse: [1] (mews).
Muslim: [1] (muslin).
muslin: [1] (Muslim).
mussel: [1] (muscle).
must: [1] (mast).
muster: [1] (musty).
musty: [1] (muster).
mutt: [1] (mud).
nave: [1] (knave).

nay: [1] (neigh).
near: [3] (knit knee no).
neat: [2] (need knead).
need: [2] (knead neat).
neigh: [1] (nay).
new: [1] (knew).
newt: [1] (nude).
next: [1] (annex).
night: [1] (knight).
no: [4] (know near knit knee).
nod: [2] (not knot).
node: [1] (note).
none: [1] (nun).
not: [2] (nod knot).
note: [1] (node).
nude: [1] (newt).
nun: [1] (none).
o: [1] (owe).
oar: [3] (or are ore).
oat: [1] (ode).
obey: [1] (abate).
odd: [2] (ought aught).
ode: [1] (oat).
of: [2] (off if).
off: [2] (of if).
office: [1] (offish).
officiate: [1] (vitiate).
officious: [1] (vicious).
offing: [1] (often).
offish: [1] (office).
often: [1] (offing).
ok: [1] (okay).
okay: [1] (ok).
omit: [2] (amid admit).
on: [2] (an in).
one: [2] (an won).
or: [9] (her heir err ere air
    were oar ore are).
orchard: [1] (archer).
ordure: [1] (orgy).
ore: [3] (or oar are).
orgy: [1] (ordure).
ought: [2] (aught odd).
our: [3] (hour how out).
out: [3] (our hour how).
overawe: [1] (overwrought).
overhand: [1] (overhang).
overhang: [1] (overhand).
overwrought: [1] (overawe).
owe: [1] (o).
packer: [1] (packet).
packet: [1] (packer).

pad: [1] (pat).
paddy: [2] (petty patty).
paid: [1] (pate).
pain: [1] (pane).
pair: [3] (pear pare pet).
panda: [1] (pander).
pander: [1] (panda).
pane: [1] (pain).
parch: [1] (porch).
pare: [3] (pear pair pet).
parity: [1] (parody).
park: [1] (pork).
parley: [1] (parlor).
parlor: [1] (parley).
parody: [1] (parity).
part: [1] (port).
partly: [1] (portly).
pass: [1] (pest).
pastor: [1] (pasty).
pasty: [1] (pastor).
pat: [1] (pad).
pate: [1] (paid).
patio: [1] (petiole).
patter: [1] (patty).
patty: [2] (patter paddy).
pawn: [1] (pond).
pea: [3] (pier peer pit).
peace: [1] (piece).
pear: [3] (pare pair pet).
pearl: [1] (purl).
peer: [3] (pea pit pier).
pellet: [1] (appellate).
pent: [1] (append).
per: [1] (purr).
pest: [1] (pass).
pet: [3] (pear pare pair).
petiole: [1] (patio).
petty: [1] (paddy).
philosopher: [1] (philosophy).
philosophy: [1] (philosopher).
picket: [1] (picky).
picky: [1] (picket).
pidgin: [1] (pigeon).
piece: [1] (peace).
pier: [3] (pea pit peer).
pigeon: [1] (pidgin).
pistil: [1] (pistol).
pistol: [1] (pistil).
pit: [3] (pier peer pea).
plaid: [1] (plat).
plain: [1] (plane).
plaintiff: [1] (plaintive).

plaintive: [1] (plaintiff).
plait: [1] (plate).
plane: [1] (plain).
plat: [2] (pled plaid).
plate: [1] (plait).
plead: [1] (pleat).
pleat: [1] (plead).
pled: [1] (plat).
plod: [2] (applaud plot).
plot: [1] (plod).
plumber: [1] (plummet).
plummet: [1] (plumber).
pod: [1] (pot).
poker: [2] (polka pokey).
pokey: [1] (poker).
polka: [1] (poker).
poll: [1] (pore).
pond: [1] (pawn).
poor: [2] (pour put).
populace: [1] (populous).
populous: [1] (populace).
porch: [1] (parch).
pore: [1] (poll).
pork: [1] (park).
port: [1] (part).
portend: [1] (pretend).
portly: [1] (partly).
pose: [1] (post).
post: [1] (pose).
pot: [1] (pod).
pour: [2] (poor put).
precede: [1] (proceed).
prescribe: [1] (proscribe).
pretend: [1] (portend).
proceed: [1] (precede).
proffer: [2] (profit prophet).
profit: [1] (proffer).
prophet: [1] (proffer).
proprietor: [1] (propriety).
propriety: [1] (proprietor).
proscribe: [1] (prescribe).
proximate: [1] (approximate).
pullet: [1] (pulley).
pulley: [1] (pullet).
purl: [1] (pearl).
purr: [1] (per).
put: [2] (pour poor).
putter: [1] (putty).
putty: [1] (putter).
quay: [2] (key kit).
queer: [1] (quit).
quid: [1] (quit).

quiet: [1] (choir).
quit: [2] (quid queer).
rabbit: [1] (rabid).
rabid: [1] (rabbit).
raid: [1] (rate).
rain: [2] (reign rein).
raise: [1] (raze).
rat: [1] (red).
ratchet: [1] (wretched).
rate: [1] (raid).
raze: [1] (raise).
read: [1] (reed).
real: [1] (rill).
rear: [1] (writ).
recede: [1] (receipt).
receipt: [1] (recede).
red: [1] (rat).
reed: [1] (read).
reign: [2] (rain rein).
rein: [2] (reign rain).
rest: [1] (wrest).
restrain: [1] (restraint).
restraint: [1] (restrain).
retard: [1] (retort).
retch: [1] (wretch).
retort: [1] (retard).
review: [1] (revue).
revue: [1] (review).
rid: [1] (writ).
ridden: [1] (written).
ride: [3] (rite right write).
rider: [1] (writer).
riding: [1] (writing).
right: [3] (ride rite write).
rill: [1] (real).
ring: [2] (wren wring).
rite: [3] (ride right write).
river: [1] (rivet).
rivet: [1] (river).
road: [3] (rote rode wrote).
roast: [1] (rose).
rocker: [1] (rocket).
rocket: [1] (rocker).
rod: [1] (rot).
rode: [3] (rote road wrote).
rood: [3] (root rude route).
root: [3] (rude rood route).
rose: [1] (roast).
rot: [1] (rod).
rote: [3] (rode road wrote).
rouble: [1] (ruble).
route: [3] (rude rood root).

ruble: [1] (rouble).
rudder: [1] (ruddy).
ruddy: [1] (rudder).
rude: [3] (root rood route).
sac: [2] (sect sack).
sack: [2] (sac sect).
sad: [1] (sat).
sadden: [1] (satin).
saddle: [1] (settle).
safe: [1] (shave).
said: [1] (set).
saint: [1] (sand).
sand: [2] (sang saint).
sane: [1] (seine).
sang: [2] (shank sand).
sat: [2] (shad sad).
sate: [1] (shade).
satin: [1] (sadden).
saw: [1] (shawl).
scar: [3] (scot Scott score).
scare: [1] (skirt).
scent: [3] (send cent sent).
score: [1] (scar).
scot: [2] (scar Scott).
Scott: [2] (scot scar).
scull: [1] (skull).
sea: [5] (sere seer sear see sit).
seam: [2] (seem sheen).
seaman: [1] (semen).
Sean: [1] (Shawn).
sear: [5] (see sea sit seer sere).
seat: [2] (seed cede).
sect: [2] (sac sack).
see: [5] (sere seer sear sea sit).
seed: [2] (cede seat).
seem: [2] (seam sheen).
seer: [5] (see sea sit sear sere).
seine: [1] (sane).
semen: [1] (seaman).
senate: [1] (synod).
send: [3] (sent scent cent).
sent: [3] (send scent cent).
sere: [5] (see sea sit seer sear).
serf: [1] (surf).
serge: [1] (surge).
set: [2] (shed said).
setter: [1] (shatter).
settle: [1] (saddle).
sewer: [1] (suet).
sewn: [1] (sown).
shad: [1] (sat).
shade: [1] (sate).

shank: [1] (sang).
shard: [1] (short).
share: [4] (shirt sir assure sure).
shatter: [1] (setter).
shave: [1] (safe).
shaven: [1] (shaving).
shaving: [1] (shaven).
shawl: [1] (saw).
Shawn: [1] (Sean).
she: [3] (cheat shear sheer).
shear: [2] (she sheer).
sheave: [1] (shift).
shed: [1] (set).
sheen: [2] (seem seam).
sheer: [2] (she shear).
sherry: [1] (surrey).
shift: [1] (sheave).
shimmer: [1] (shimmy).
shimmy: [1] (shimmer).
shiner: [1] (shiny).
shiny: [1] (shiner).
shirt: [5] (should share sir
  assure sure).
shod: [1] (shot).
shone: [1] (shown).
shoot: [1] (chute).
shore: [1] (short).
short: [2] (shard shore).
shot: [1] (shod).
should: [3] (shirt soot sure).
shout: [2] (sow sough).
shown: [1] (shone).
shudder: [1] (shutter).
shun: [2] (sum some).
shutter: [1] (shudder).
side: [3] (sight cite site).
sieve: [1] (sift).
sift: [1] (sieve).
sight: [3] (cite side site).
sink: [1] (sync).
sir: [4] (shirt share assure sure).
sit: [5] (sere seer sear see sea).
site: [3] (sight cite side).
ski: [1] (skit).
skid: [1] (skit).
skirt: [1] (scare).
skit: [2] (skid ski).
skull: [1] (scull).
slang: [1] (slant).
slant: [1] (slang).
slat: [1] (sled).
slay: [1] (sleigh).

sled: [1] (slat).
sleigh: [1] (slay).
sleight: [2] (slide slight).
slew: [1] (slough).
slid: [1] (slit).
slide: [2] (slight sleight).
slight: [2] (slide sleight).
slit: [1] (slid).
slough: [1] (slew).
snore: [1] (snort).
snort: [1] (snore).
soar: [2] (sort sore).
soccer: [1] (socket).
socket: [1] (soccer).
sod: [1] (sot).
sofa: [1] (chauffeur).
sol: [2] (sole soul).
solar: [1] (solely).
sole: [2] (sol soul).
solely: [1] (solar).
some: [2] (sum shun).
soon: [1] (assume).
soot: [1] (should).
sore: [2] (soar sort).
sort: [3] (sword soar sore).
sot: [1] (sod).
sough: [2] (sow shout).
soul: [2] (sole sol).
sow: [2] (sough shout).
sown: [1] (sewn).
spade: [1] (spate).
span: [2] (spend spent).
spar: [2] (spoor spore).
spat: [1] (sped).
spate: [1] (spade).
spear: [1] (spit).
sped: [1] (spat).
spend: [2] (span spent).
spent: [2] (spend span).
spit: [1] (spear).
spoon: [1] (spume).
spoor: [2] (spar spore).
spore: [2] (spar spoor).
sprat: [1] (spread).
spread: [1] (sprat).
spring: [1] (sprint).
sprint: [1] (spring).
spume: [1] (spoon).
squad: [1] (squat).
square: [1] (squirt).
squat: [1] (squad).
squirt: [1] (square).

staid: [1] (state).
stair: [1] (stare).
stake: [1] (steak).
stanch: [1] (staunch).
star: [1] (store).
stare: [1] (stair).
state: [1] (staid).
stationary: [1] (stationery).
stationery: [1] (stationary).
staunch: [1] (stanch).
steak: [1] (stake).
step: [1] (steppe).
steppe: [1] (step).
stile: [1] (style).
sting: [1] (stint).
stint: [1] (sting).
store: [1] (star).
straight: [1] (strait).
straighten: [1] (straiten).
strait: [1] (straight).
straiten: [1] (straighten).
stringer: [1] (stringy).
stringy: [1] (stringer).
sty: [1] (stye).
stye: [1] (sty).
style: [1] (stile).
stylish: [1] (stylus).
stylist: [1] (stylus).
stylus: [2] (stylist stylish).
subtile: [1] (subtle).
subtle: [1] (subtile).
suet: [1] (sewer).
suite: [2] (swede sweet).
sum: [2] (some shun).
summer: [1] (summit).
summit: [1] (summer).
sundae: [1] (Sunday).
Sunday: [2] (sundae sunder).
sunder: [1] (Sunday).
sure: [6] (your shirt share sir
    assure should).
surely: [1] (surly).
surf: [1] (serf).
surge: [1] (serge).
surly: [1] (surely).
surrey: [1] (sherry).
sward: [2] (swart swore).
swart: [2] (sward swore).
swear: [1] (sweat).
sweat: [1] (swear).
swede: [2] (sweet suite).
sweet: [2] (swede suite).

sword: [1] (sort).
swore: [2] (swart sward).
sync: [1] (sink).
synod: [1] (senate).
taint: [2] (tan attain).
tan: [2] (attain taint).
taper: [1] (tapir).
tapir: [1] (taper).
tar: [4] (toward tort tore tot).
tare: [2] (to tear).
tarn: [1] (torn).
tart: [1] (toward).
taught: [1] (taut).
taunt: [1] (tong).
taut: [1] (taught).
tax: [1] (text).
tea: [6] (tit teat tier tear tee to).
tear: [7] (tit teat tee tea to tier tare).
teat: [6] (tit tier tear tee tea to).
tee: [6] (tit teat tier tear tea to).
tend: [1] (tint).
tenet: [1] (tenor).
tenor: [2] (tinder tenet).
tern: [1] (turn).
tester: [1] (testy).
testy: [1] (tester).
text: [1] (tax).
thane: [1] (thegn).
the: [6] (they though thee we he eat).
thee: [3] (they though the).
thegn: [1] (thane).
their: [2] (there they're).
then: [5] (in end Anne Ann an).
there: [2] (their they're).
they: [3] (thee the though).
they're: [2] (there their).
this: [1] (is).
thole: [1] (though).
though: [4] (thole they thee the).
thread: [1] (threat).
threat: [1] (thread).
throne: [1] (thrown).
thrown: [1] (throne).
tide: [1] (tight).
tier: [6] (tit teat tee tea to tear).
tight: [1] (tide).
tinder: [1] (tenor).
tint: [1] (tend).
tit: [6] (teat tier tear tee tea to).
to: [8] (tare tour tit teat tier tear
     tee tea).
toad: [1] (tote).

tocsin: [1] (toxin).
Todd: [1] (tot).
ton: [1] (tun).
tong: [1] (taunt).
Torah: [1] (Tory).
tore: [3] (toward tort tar).
torn: [1] (tarn).
tort: [3] (toward tar tore).
Tory: [1] (Torah).
tot: [2] (Todd tar).
tote: [1] (toad).
tour: [1] (to).
toward: [4] (tort tar tore tart).
toxin: [1] (tocsin).
trade: [1] (trait).
trader: [1] (traitor).
trait: [1] (trade).
traitor: [1] (trader).
trod: [1] (trot).
trot: [1] (trod).
tsar: [1] (czar).
tun: [1] (ton).
turban: [1] (turbine).
turbid: [1] (turbot).
turbine: [1] (turban).
turbot: [1] (turbid).
turn: [1] (tern).
tweed: [1] (tweet).
tweet: [1] (tweed).
urn: [1] (earn).
us: [1] (ass).
vague: [1] (fag).
vail: [1] (veil).
vain: [2] (vane vein).
van: [2] (vend vent).
vane: [2] (vain vein).
vary: [1] (very).
vector: [1] (factor).
very: [1] (ferry).
veil: [1] (vail).
vein: [2] (vane vain).
veldt: [1] (felt).
vend: [2] (van vent).
vender: [1] (vendor).
vendor: [1] (vender).
venous: [1] (Venus).
vent: [3] (fend vend van).
Venus: [1] (venous).
verse: [1] (first).
very: [1] (vary).
vessel: [1] (facile).
vest: [1] (fast).

vet: [2] (fed fat).
vice: [1] (vise).
vicious: [1] (officious).
vier: [1] (fire).
villa: [1] (filler).
vim: [2] (Finn fin).
viol: [1] (file).
viscous: [1] (viscus).
viscus: [1] (viscous).
vise: [1] (vice).
vitiate: [1] (officiate).
viva: [1] (fever).
voice: [1] (foist).
vole: [2] (fold vote).
volt: [1] (fold).
vote: [1] (vole).
wabble: [1] (wobble).
wad: [1] (watt).
waddle: [1] (wattle).
wade: [2] (wait weight).
waist: [1] (waste).
wait: [2] (wade weight).
waiver: [2] (wavy waver).
wand: [2] (want wont).
want: [2] (wand wont).
ware: [4] (weird weir wear wet).
wary: [3] (worry wherry wearer).
was: [2] (is as).
washer: [1] (washy).
washy: [1] (washer).
waste: [1] (waist).
watt: [1] (wad).
wattle: [1] (waddle).
waver: [2] (wavy waiver).
wavy: [2] (waver waiver).
we: [6] (he eat the wit with wee).
we'll: [1] (will).
wean: [1] (ween).
wear: [4] (weird weir ware wet).
wearer: [1] (wary).
weather: [2] (wether whether).
wed: [1] (wet).
wee: [3] (wit with we).
weed: [1] (wheat).
ween: [1] (wean).
weeny: [1] (wiener).
weight: [2] (wade wait).
weir: [4] (weird wear ware wet).
weird: [3] (weir wear ware).
weld: [1] (welt).
welt: [1] (weld).
went: [1] (wind).

were: [7] (or her are heir err ere air).
wet: [4] (wed weir wear ware).
wether: [2] (weather whether).
wheat: [1] (weed).
wheel: [1] (wield).
where: [1] (whet).
wherry: [1] (wary).
whet: [1] (where).
whether: [2] (wether weather).
whim: [1] (win).
whirl: [1] (world).
whisker: [1] (whisky).
whisky: [1] (whisker).
whist: [1] (whizz).
whizz: [1] (whist).
wholly: [1] (holy).
why: [2] (wight wire).
wicked: [1] (wicket).
wicker: [1] (wicket).
wicket: [2] (wicked wicker).
wide: [1] (wight).
wield: [2] (wilt wheel).
wiener: [1] (weeny).
wight: [3] (wide why wire).
will: [1] (we'll).
wilt: [1] (wield).
win: [1] (whim).
wind: [1] (went).
wire: [2] (wight why).
wit: [3] (wee we with).
with: [3] (wit wee we).
wobble: [1] (wabble).
won: [1] (one).
wont: [2] (wand want).
wood: [1] (would).
wooden: [1] (wouldn't).
word: [1] (wort).
world: [1] (whirl).
worry: [1] (wary).
worst: [1] (wurst).
wort: [1] (word).
would: [1] (wood).
wouldn't: [1] (wooden).
wren: [2] (ring wring).
wrest: [1] (rest).
wretch: [1] (retch).
wretched: [1] (ratchet).
wring: [2] (wren ring).
writ: [2] (rid rear).
write: [3] (ride rite right).
writer: [1] (rider).
writing: [1] (riding).

written: [1] (ridden).
wrote: [3] (rode road rote).
wurst: [1] (worst).
yard: [1] (your).
yawl: [1] (your).

you: [1] (your).
your: [7] (jar yard yawl you chore char sure).
Zen: [1] (zing).
zing: [1] (Zen).

References

Abū Raihān al-Bīrūnī. 1030. *An Accurate Description of All Categories of Hindu Thought*. In J.F. Stall (ed.), *A Reader on the Sanskrit Grammarians*. Cambridge: The MIT Press, 1972.

Anderson, Stephen R. 1985. *Phonology in the Twentieth Century*. Chicago: The University of Chicago Press.

Baayen, Harald. 1991. A stochastic process for word frequency distributions. *Proceedings of the 29th Meeting of the Association for Computational Linguistics.*, pp. 271–78.

Bahl, L.R., R. Bakis, P.S. Cohen, A.G. Cole, F. Jelinek, B.L. Lewis, and R.L. Mercer. 1979. Recognition results with several experimental acoustic processors, *Proceedings of the IEEE International Conference on Acoustics, Speech, and Signal Processing*, pp. 249–51.

Bahl, L.R., R. Bakis, P.S. Cohen, A.G. Cole, F. Jelinek, B.L. Lewis, and R.L. Mercer. 1980. Further results on the recognition of a continuously read natural corpus. *Proceedings of the IEEE International Conference on Acoustics, Speech, and Signal Processing*, pp. 872–75.

Bahl, L.R., P.V. de Souza, P.S. Gopalakrishnan, D. Nahamoo, and M.A. Picheny. 1991. Context dependent modeling of phones in continuous speech using decisions trees. *Proceedings of the 4th DARPA Speech and Natural Language Workshop*. San Mateo: Morgan Kaufmann Publishers, pp. 264–69.

Baker, J. 1975. The DRAGON system–an overview, *IEEE Transactions on Acoustics, Speech, and Signal Processing* **23**, pp. 24–29.

Barton, G., R. Berwick, and E. Ristad. 1987. *Computational Complexity and Natural Language*. Cambridge, MA: The MIT Press.

Baudouin de Courtenay, Jan. 1972. An Attempt at a Theory of Phonetic Alternations. In *A Baudouin de Courtenay Anthology*. Translated by Edward Stankiewicz. Bloomington, IN: Indiana University Press.

Baum, L., T. Petrie, G. Soules, and N. Weiss. 1970. A maximization technique occurring in the statistical analysis of probabilistic functions of Markov chains, *Ann. Math Statistics* **41**(1), pp. 164–71.

Bell, T., D. Dirks and E. Carterette. 1989. Interactive factors in consonant confusion patterns, *J. Acoust. Soc. Am.* **85**(1), pp. 339–46.

Bishop, Y.M.M., S.E. Fienberg, and P.W. Holland. 1977. *Discrete Multivariate Analysis: Theory and Practice*. Cambridge, MA: MIT Press, third printing.

Breiman, L., J.H. Friedman, R.A. Olshen, and C.J. Stone. 1984. *Classification and Regression Trees*. Belmont: Wadsworth International Group.

Carter, David M. 1987. An information-theoretic analysis of phonetic dictionary access. *Computer Speech and Language* **2**, pp. 1–11.

Chen F. 1985. *Acoustic-Phonetic Constraints in Continuous Speech Recognition: A Case Study Using the Digit Vocabulary*. Ph.D. Dissertation, Massachusetts Institute of Technology, Cambridge, MA.

Chen, F., and J. Shrager. 1989. Automatic discovery of contextual rules describing phonological variation. *Proceedings of the DARPA Speech and Natural Language Workshop*. San Mateo: Morgan Kaufmann Publishers, pp. 284–89.

Chen, F. 1990. Identification of contextual factors for pronunciation networks. *Proceedings of the IEEE International Conference on Acoustics, Speech, and Signal Processing*, pp. 753–56.

Chen, F.R. and M.M. Withgott. 1992. The use of emphasis to automatically summarize a spoken discourse. *Proceedings of the IEEE International Conference on Acoustics, Speech and Signal Processing*, pp. 229–33.

Chomsky, Noam and Morris Halle. 1968. *The Sound Pattern of English*. New York: Harper and Row.

Chou, P. 1988. *Applications of Information Theory to Pattern Recognition and the Design of Decision Trees and Trellises*. PhD. Dissertation, Stanford University, Stanford, CA.

Chow, Y., R. Schwartz, S. Roucos, O. Kimball, P. Price, R. Kubala, M. Dunham, M. Krasner, and J. Makhoul. 1986. The role of word-dependent coarticulatory effects in a phoneme-based speech recognition system. *Proceedings of the IEEE International Conference on Acoustics, Speech and Signal Processing*, pp. 1593–96.

Cohen, Michael Harris. 1989. *Phonological Structures for Speech Recognition*. Ph.D. Dissertation, University of California, Berkeley, CA.

Cohen, P.S. and P.L. Mercer. 1975. The phonological component of an automatic speech recognition system. In R. Reddy (ed.), *Speech Recognition*. New York: Academic Press. pp. 275–320.

Cooke, Perry. 1990. *Identification of Control Parameters in an Articulatory Vocal Tract Model, with Applications to the Synthesis of Singing*. Ph.D. Dissertation, Stanford University, Stanford, CA.

Fant, Gunnar. 1973. *Speech Sounds and Features*. Cambridge, MA: MIT Press.

Fant, Gunnar. 1990. The role of speech research in the advance of speech technology. Stockholm: *Speech Transmission Laboratory Quarterly Progress and Status Report* 4, pp. 1–7.

Fienberg, Stephen E. 1985. The analysis of cross-classified categorical data. Cambridge, MA: MIT Press, fourth printing.

Fisher, W., V. Zue, J. Bernstein, and D. Pallett. 1987. An acoustic-phonetic data base. *J. Acoust. Soc. Am.*, Suppl. 1, **81**.

Francis, W.N. and F. Kucera. 1982. *Frequency Analysis of English Usage*. Boston: Houghton Mifflin.

Gallager, R. 1968. *Information Theory and Reliable Communication*. New York: John Wiley and Sons.

Ganapathy, S. and V. Rajaraman. 1973. Information theory applied to the conversion of decision tables to computer programs. *Commun. of the ACM*, **16**(9), pp. 532–39.

Halle, M. and M. Kenstowicz. 1991. The free element condition and cyclic versus noncyclic stress. *Linguistic Inquiry* **22**(3), pp. 457–501.

Halle, M. and K.P. Mohanan. 1985. Segmental phonology of modern English. *Linguistic Inquiry* **16**(1), pp. 57–116.

Harrington, Jonathan and Anne Johnstone. 1987. The effects of equivalence classes on parsing phonemes into words in continuous speech recognition. *Computer, Speech and Language* **22**, pp. 273–88.

Henrichon, J. and K. Fu. 1969. A nonparametric partitioning procedure for pattern classification. *IEEE Transactions on Computers* **C-18**, pp. 614–24.

Hogg, T. and J. Kephart. 1988. Phase transitions in high-dimensional pattern classification. *Xerox Technical Report* P88-00102.

Hopcroft, John and John Ullman. 1969. *Introduction to Automata Theory, Languages, and Computation*. Reading, MA: Addison-Wesley.

Huttenlocher, D.P. 1985. Exploiting Sequential Constraints in Recognizing Spoken Words. MIT A.I. Memo 867.

Huttenlocher, D.P. and V.W. Zue. 1983. Phonotactic and Lexical Constraints in Speech Recognition. *Proceedings of the National Conference on Artificial Intelligence*, AAAI83, Washington D.C., pp. 172–76.

Hunnicutt, Sheri. 1987. Input and Output Alternatives in Word Prediction. *STL-QPSR*. Royal Institute of Technology, Stockholm **2–3**, pp. 15–30.

Jakobson, Roman, Gunnar Fant, and Morris Halle. 1952. *Preliminaries to Speech Analysis*. *Technical Report 13, Acoustics Laboratory*, MIT Cambridge, MA.

Jakobson, Roman and Krystyna Pomorska. 1983. *Dialogues*. Cambridge, MA.: MIT Press.

Jelinek, F. 1985. The Development of an Experimental Discrete Dictation Recognizer. *Proceedings of the IEEE* **73**(11), pp. 1616–24.

Jelinek, F. 1985. Self-Organized Language Modeling for Speech Recognition. IBM Research Report. T.J. Watson Research Center, Yorktown Heights, NY. (Also available in Waibel and Lee (eds.), *Readings in Speech Recognition*. San Mateo, CA: Morgan Kaufmann, 1990.)

Jelinek F. and R. Mercer. 1980. Interpolated estimation of Markov source parameters from sparse data. In E. Gelsema and L. Kanal (eds.), *Proceedings of Pattern Recognition in Practice Workshop*, North-Holland, pp. 381–97.

Kahn, Daniel. 1976. *Syllable-Based Generalizations in English Phonology*. Ph.D. Dissertation, MIT, Cambridge, MA. Reproduced by Indiana University Linguistics Club, Bloomington, IN.

Kaplan, Ronlad M. and Martin Kay. 1981. Phonological rules and finite-state transducers. Paper presented to the Winter meeting of the Linguistic Society of America. New York, New York.

Karttunen, Lauri. 1983. KIMMO: A General Morphological Processor. The University of Texas, Austin, Texas: *Texas Linguistic Forum 22*. pp. 167–86.

Koskenniemi, Kimmo. 1983. *Two-level morphology: A general computational model for word-form recognition and production*. Ph.D. Dissertation, University of Helsinki, Helsinki, Finland.

Koskenniemi, Kimmo. 1983. *Two-level model for morphological analysis*. *IJCAI-83*, Karlsruhe, Germany. pp. 683–85.

Kiparsky, Paul. 1968. How abstract is phonology? Department of Linguistics and Philosophy, MIT, Cambridge, MA. Reprinted in O. Fujimura (ed.), *Three Dimensions of Linguistic Theory*. Tokyo: The TEC Corporation. pp. 57–86.

Kiparsky, Paul. 1979. Metrical Structure Assignment is Cyclic. *Linguistic Inquiry*, **10**(3), pp. 421–42.

Kiparsky, Paul. 1981. Lexical Morphology and Phonology. In I.-S. Yang, (ed.). *Linguistics in the Morning Calm*. Seoul, Korea: Hanshin.

Kisseberth, Charles W. 1973. Is Rule Ordering Necessary? In Krachu et al. (eds.), *Issues in Linguistics, Papers in Honor of Henry and Renee Kahane*. Urbana, IL: University of Illinois Press.

Koutsoudas, Andreas, Gerald Sanders and Craig Noll. 1974. The Application of Phonological Rules. *Language* **50**(1), pp. 1–28.

Kuhn, R. 1988. Speech Recognition and the Frequency of Recently Used Words: a Modified Markov Model for Natural Language. *Proceedings of COLING, Budapest* **1**, pp. 348–50.

Kupiec, J. 1989. Probabilistic Models of Short and Long Distance Word Dependencies in Running Text. *Proceedings of the DARPA Speech and Natural Language Workshop.* San Mateo: Morgan Kaufmann Publishers. pp. 290–95.

Kurath, Hans. 1939. *Handbook of the Linguistic Geography of New England.* Providence, Rhode Island: Brown University.

Labov, William. 1972. *Sociolinguistic Patterns.* Philadelphia: University of Pennsylvania Press.

Ladefoged, Peter. 1975. *A Course in Phonetics.* New York: Harcourt Brace Jovanovich, Inc.

Lamel, Lori F., Robert H. Kassel, and Stephanie Seneff. 1986. Speech database development: Design and analysis of the acoustic-phonetic corpus. *Proceedings of the* DARPA *Speech Recognition Workshop.* Palo Alto, CA.

Landauer, T.K. and L.A. Streeter. 1973. Structural differences between common and rare words: Failure of equivalence assumptions for theories of word recognition. *J. Verbal Learning Behavior* **12**, pp. 119–31.

Lee, K.F. 1988. *Large-Vocabulary Speaker-Independent Continuous Speech Recognition: The SPHINX System.* Ph.D. Dissertation, Carnegie Mellon University, Pittsburgh, PA.

Lee, K-F., H.-W. Hon, M.-Y. Hwang, S. Mahajan, R. Reddy. 1989. The SPHINX speech recognition system. *Proceedings of the* IEEE *International Conference on Acoustics, Speech, and Signal Processing,* pp. 445–48.

Lee, K.F., S. Hayamizu, H.-W. Hon, C. Huang, J. Swartz and R. Weide. 1990. Allophone clustering for continuous speech recognition. *Proceedings of the IEEE International Conference on Acoustics, Speech and Signal Processing,* pp. 749–52.

Leonard, R.G. 1984. A database for speaker-independent digit recognition. *Proceedings of the IEEE International Conference on Acoustics, Speech and Signal Processing,* pp. 42.11.1–42.11.4.

Leung, H., V. Zue. 1984. A procedure for automatic alignment of phonetic transcriptions with continuous speech. *Proceedings of the IEEE International Conference on Acoustics, Speech and Signal Processing,* pp. 2.7.1–2.7.4.

Levinson, S., L. Rabiner, and M. Sondhi. 1983. An introduction to the application of the theory of probabilistic functions of a Markov process to automatic speech recognition. *Bell System Technical Journal* **62**(4), Part 1, pp. 1035-74.

Liberman, M. and A. Prince. 1977. On Stress and Linguistic Rhythm. *Linguistic Inquiry* **8**, pp. 249-336.

Lowerre, B. 1976. *The HARPY Speech Recognition System*. Ph.D. Dissertation, Carnegie Mellon University, Pittsburgh, PA.

Luce, R.D. R. Bush, and E. Galanter (eds.) 1965. *Readings in Mathematical Psychology*. New York: John Wiley and Sons.

Luce, Paul A. 1986. *Neighborhoods of words in the mental lexicon*. Ph.D. Dissertation, Indiana University, Bloomington, IN.

Malmberg, Bertil. 1967. The Phonetic Basis for Syllable Division. In Lehiste (ed.), *Readings in Acoustic Phonetics*. Cambridge, MA: MIT Press.

Massaro, D.W. 1972. Perceptual images, processing time, and perceptual units in auditory perception. *Psychological Review*, **79**, pp. 124-145.

Marslen-Wilson, William, and A. Welsh. 1978. Processing interactions and lexical access during word recognition in continuous speech. *Cognitive Psychology*, **10**, pp. 29-63.

McMillan, Clayton, Michael C. Mozer, and Paul Smolensky. 1991. The Connectionist Scientist Game: Rule Extraction and Refinement in a Neural Network. In *Proceedings of the Thirteenth Annual Conference of the Cognitive Science Society*.

Mercer, Robert. 1988. Language modelling for speech recognition. Presentation at 1988 IEEE Workshop on Speech Recognition. Arden House, Harriman, NY. May 31-June 3.

Mohanan, K.P. 1982. *Lexical Phonology*. Ph.D. Dissertation, MIT, Cambridge, MA.

Murveit, H., M. Cohen, P. Price, G. Baldwin, M. Weintraub, and J. Bernstein. 1989. SRI's DECIPHER system. *Proceedings February 1989 Speech and Natural Language Workshop*. San Mateo: Morgan Kaufmann Publishers. pp. 238-42.

Paul, D. and E. Martin. 1988. Speaker stress-resistant continuous speech recognizer. *Proceedings of the IEEE International Conference on Acoustics, Speech and Signal Processing*, pp. 283-86.

Paul, D.B. 1989. The Lincoln robust continuous speech recognizer. *Proceedings of the IEEE International Conference on Acoustics, Speech and Signal Processing*, pp. 449-52.

Paul, D.B. 1990. The Lincoln tied-mixture HMM continuous speech recognizer. *Proceedings June 1990 Speech and Natural Language Workshop*. San Mateo: Morgan Kaufmann Publishers. pp. 332-36.

Payne, Harold J. and William S. Meisel. 1977. An algorithm for constructing optimal binary decision trees. *IEEE Transactions on Computers.* pp. 905–16.

Peet, Margot. 1988. *Postlexical Palatalization in English: An Acoustic-Phonetic Study.* Ph.D. Dissertation, U.C. Berkeley, Berkeley, CA.

Pelletier, Francis Jeffry. 1980. The generative power of rule orderings in formal grammars. *Linguistics* **18**(1), pp. 17–72.

Pinker, S. and A. Prince. 1988. On language and connectionism: Analysis of a parellel distributed processing model of language acquisition. *Cognition*, **28**, pp. 73–193.

Pisoni, D. 1977. Identification and discrimination of the relative onset time of two component tones: Implications for voicing perception in stops. *Journal of the Acoustical Society of America* 61, pp. 1352–61.

Poritz, Alan B. 1988. Hidden Markov models: A guided tour. *Proceedings of the IEEE International Conference on Acoustics, Speech, and Signal Processing*, pp. 7–13.

Quinlan, J.R. 1986. Induction of decision trees. *Machine Learning* **1**, pp. 1–86. Boston: Kluwer Academic Publishers.

Quinlan, J.R. 1987. Generating production rules from decision trees. *Proceedings of the Tenth International Joint Conference on Artificial Intelligence*, pp. 304–07.

Rabiner, L. and B. Juang. 1986. An introduction to hidden Markov models. *IEEE ASSP Magazine*, **3**(1), pp. 4–16.

Riley, M.D. 1989. Some applications of tree-based modelling to speech and language. *Proceedings of the DARPA Speech and Natural Language Workshop.* San Mateo: Morgan Kaufmann Publishers. pp. 339–52.

Rumelhart, D.E. and J.L. McClelland. 1986. On learning the past tenses of English verbs. In *Parallel Distributed Processing: Explorations in the Microstructure of Cognition.* Cambridge, MA: MIT Press.

Sagayama, S. 1989. Phoneme environment clustering for speech recognition. *Proceedings of the IEEE International Conference on Acoustics, Speech and Signal Processing*, pp. 397–400.

Scarborough, D., C. Cortese, and H. Scarborough. 1977. Frequency and repetition effects in lexical memory. *Journal of Experimental Psychology: Human Perception and Performance*, **3**, pp. 1–17.

Shipman, D. and V.W. Zue. 1982. Properties of large lexicons: implications for advanced isolated word recognition systems. *Proceedings of the International Conference on Acoustics, Speech and Signal Processing*, pp. 546–49.

Simpson, J. and M. Withgott. 1986. Pronominal Clitic Clusters and

Templates. In H. Borer (ed.), *Syntax and Semantics, The Syntax of Pronominal Clitics*, **19**, pp. 149–73.

Stampe, D. 1973. *A Dissertation on Natural Phonology*. Ph.D. Dissertation, Department of Linguistics, The University of Chicago, Chicago.

Touretzky, David S. 1989. Rules and Maps in Connectionist Symbol Processing. *Technical Report CMU-CS-89-158*, Carnegie Mellon University, Pittsburgh, PA.

Viterbi, Andrew J. and Jim K. Omura. 1979. *Principles of Digital Communication and Coding*. New York: McGraw-Hill Book Company.

Wasow, T. 1978. On Constraining the Class of Transformational Languages. *Synthese* **39**. pp. 181–204. Reprinted in E. Bach, W. Marsh, and W. Savitch (eds.), *The Formal Complexity of Natural Language*. Dordrecht, The Netherlands: Reidel.

Withgott, M. 1982. *Segmental Evidence for Phonological Constituents*. Ph.D. Dissertation, Department of Linguistics, The University of Texas, Austin, TX. (Available from University Microfilms, Ann Arbor, MI.)

Weintraub, M., H. Murveit, M. Cohen, P. Price, J. Bernstein, G. Baldwin, and D. Bell. 1989. Linguistic constraints in hidden Markov model based speech recognition. *Proceedings of the IEEE International Conference on Acoustics, Speech, and Signal Processing*, pp. 699–702.

Zipf, G.K. 1935. *The Psycho-Biology of Language*. Boston: Houghton Mifflin.

Index

CSLI Publications

Reports

The following titles have been published in the CSLI Reports series. These reports may be obtained from CSLI Publications, Ventura Hall, Stanford, CA 94305-4115.

Coordination and How to Distinguish Categories Ivan Sag, Gerald Gazdar, Thomas Wasow, and Steven Weisler CSLI-84-3

Belief and Incompleteness Kurt Konolige CSLI-84-4

Equality, Types, Modules and Generics for Logic Programming Joseph Goguen and José Meseguer CSLI-84-5

Lessons from Bolzano Johan van Benthem CSLI-84-6

Self-propagating Search: A Unified Theory of Memory Pentti Kanerva CSLI-84-7

Reflection and Semantics in LISP Brian Cantwell Smith CSLI-84-8

The Implementation of Procedurally Reflective Languages Jim des Rivières and Brian Cantwell Smith CSLI-84-9

Parameterized Programming Joseph Goguen CSLI-84-10

Shifting Situations and Shaken Attitudes Jon Barwise and John Perry CSLI-84-13

Completeness of Many-Sorted Equational Logic Joseph Goguen and José Meseguer CSLI-84-15

Moving the Semantic Fulcrum Terry Winograd CSLI-84-17

On the Mathematical Properties of Linguistic Theories C. Raymond Perrault CSLI-84-18

A Simple and Efficient Implementation of Higher-order Functions in LISP Michael P. Georgeff and Stephen F. Bodnar CSLI-84-19

On the Axiomatization of "if-then-else" Irène Guessarian and José Meseguer CSLI-85-20

The Situation in Logic–II: Conditionals and Conditional Information Jon Barwise CSLI-84-21

Principles of OBJ2 Kokichi Futatsugi, Joseph A. Goguen, Jean-Pierre Jouannaud, and José Meseguer CSLI-85-22

Querying Logical Databases Moshe Vardi CSLI-85-23

Computationally Relevant Properties of Natural Languages and Their Grammar Gerald Gazdar and Geoff Pullum CSLI-85-24

An Internal Semantics for Modal Logic: Preliminary Report Ronald Fagin and Moshe Vardi CSLI-85-25

The Situation in Logic–III: Situations, Sets and the Axiom of Foundation Jon Barwise CSLI-85-26

Semantic Automata Johan van Benthem CSLI-85-27

Restrictive and Non-Restrictive Modification Peter Sells CSLI-85-28

Institutions: Abstract Model Theory for Computer Science J. A. Goguen and R. M. Burstall CSLI-85-30

A Formal Theory of Knowledge and Action Robert C. Moore CSLI-85-31

Finite State Morphology: A Review of Koskenniemi (1983) Gerald Gazdar CSLI-85-32

The Role of Logic in Artificial Intelligence Robert C. Moore CSLI-85-33

Applicability of Indexed Grammars to Natural Languages Gerald Gazdar CSLI-85-34

Commonsense Summer: Final Report Jerry R. Hobbs, et al CSLI-85-35

Limits of Correctness in Computers Brian Cantwell Smith CSLI-85-36

The Coherence of Incoherent Discourse Jerry R. Hobbs and Michael H. Agar CSLI-85-38

A Complete, Type-free "Second-order" Logic and Its Philosophical Foundations Christopher Menzel CSLI-86-40

Possible-world Semantics for Autoepistemic Logic Robert C. Moore CSLI-85-41

Deduction with Many-Sorted Rewrite José Meseguer and Joseph A. Goguen CSLI-85-42

Lecture Notes

The titles in this series are distributed by the University of Chicago Press and may be purchased in academic or university bookstores or ordered directly from the distributor at 11030 South Langley Avenue, Chicago, IL 60628 (USA) or by phone 1-800-621-2736, (312)568-1550.

A Manual of Intensional Logic. Johan van Benthem, second edition, revised and expanded. Lecture Notes No. 1. 0-937073-29-6 (paper), 0-937073-30-X (cloth)

Emotion and Focus. Helen Fay Nissenbaum. Lecture Notes No. 2. 0-937073-20-2 (paper)

Lectures on Contemporary Syntactic Theories. Peter Sells. Lecture Notes No. 3. 0-937073-14-8 (paper), 0-937073-13-X (cloth)

An Introduction to Unification-Based Approaches to Grammar. Stuart M. Shieber. Lecture Notes No. 4. 0-937073-00-8 (paper), 0-937073-01-6 (cloth)

The Semantics of Destructive Lisp. Ian A. Mason. Lecture Notes No. 5. 0-937073-06-7 (paper), 0-937073-05-9 (cloth)

An Essay on Facts. Ken Olson. Lecture Notes No. 6. 0-937073-08-3 (paper), 0-937073-05-9 (cloth)

Logics of Time and Computation. Robert Goldblatt, second edition, revised and expanded. Lecture Notes No. 7. 0-937073-94-6 (paper), 0-937073-93-8 (cloth)

Word Order and Constituent Structure in German. Hans Uszkoreit. Lecture Notes No. 8. 0-937073-10-5 (paper), 0-937073-09-1 (cloth)

Color and Color Perception: A Study in Anthropocentric Realism. David Russel Hilbert. Lecture Notes No. 9. 0-937073-16-4 (paper), 0-937073-15-6 (cloth)

Prolog and Natural-Language Analysis. Fernando C. N. Pereira and Stuart M. Shieber. Lecture Notes No. 10. 0-937073-18-0 (paper), 0-937073-17-2 (cloth)

Working Papers in Grammatical Theory and Discourse Structure: Interactions of Morphology, Syntax, and Discourse. M. Iida, S. Wechsler, and D. Zec (Eds.) with an Introduction by Joan Bresnan. Lecture Notes No. 11. 0-937073-04-0 (paper), 0-937073-25-3 (cloth)

Natural Language Processing in the 1980s: A Bibliography. Gerald Gazdar, Alex Franz, Karen Osborne, and Roger Evans. Lecture Notes No. 12. 0-937073-28-8 (paper), 0-937073-26-1 (cloth)

Information-Based Syntax and Semantics. Carl Pollard and Ivan Sag. Lecture Notes No. 13. 0-937073-24-5 (paper), 0-937073-23-7 (cloth)

Non-Well-Founded Sets. Peter Aczel. Lecture Notes No. 14. 0-937073-22-9 (paper), 0-937073-21-0 (cloth)

Partiality, Truth and Persistence. Tore Langholm. Lecture Notes No. 15. 0-937073-34-2 (paper), 0-937073-35-0 (cloth)

Attribute-Value Logic and the Theory of Grammar. Mark Johnson. Lecture Notes No. 16. 0-937073-36-9 (paper), 0-937073-37-7 (cloth)

The Situation in Logic. Jon Barwise. Lecture Notes No. 17. 0-937073-32-6 (paper), 0-937073-33-4 (cloth)

The Linguistics of Punctuation. Geoff Nunberg. Lecture Notes No. 18. 0-937073-46-6 (paper), 0-937073-47-4 (cloth)

Anaphora and Quantification in Situation Semantics. Jean Mark Gawron and Stanley Peters. Lecture Notes No. 19. 0-937073-48-4 (paper), 0-937073-49-0 (cloth)

Propositional Attitudes: The Role of Content in Logic, Language, and Mind. C. Anthony Anderson and Joseph Owens. Lecture Notes No. 20. 0-937073-50-4 (paper), 0-937073-51-2 (cloth)

Literature and Cognition. Jerry R. Hobbs. Lecture Notes No. 21. 0-937073-52-0 (paper), 0-937073-53-9 (cloth)

Situation Theory and Its Applications, Vol. 1. Robin Cooper, Kuniaki Mukai, and John Perry (Eds.). Lecture Notes No. 22. 0-937073-54-7 (paper), 0-937073-55-5 (cloth)

The Language of First-Order Logic (including the Macintosh program, Tarski's World). Jon Barwise and John Etchemendy, second edition, revised and expanded. Lecture Notes No. 23. 0-937073-74-1 (paper)

Lexical Matters. Ivan A. Sag and Anna Szabolcsi, editors. Lecture Notes No. 24. 0-937073-66-0 (paper), 0-937073-65-2 (cloth)

Tarski's World. Jon Barwise and John Etchemendy. Lecture Notes No. 25. 0-937073-67-9 (paper)

Situation Theory and Its Applications, Vol. 2. Jon Barwise, J. Mark Gawron, Gordon Plotkin, Syun Tutiya, editors. Lecture Notes No. 26. 0-937073-70-9 (paper), 0-937073-71-7 (cloth)

Literate Programming. Donald E. Knuth. Lecture Notes No. 27. 0-937073-80-6 (paper), 0-937073-81-4 (cloth)

Normalization, Cut-Elimination and the Theory of Proofs. A. M. Ungar. Lecture Notes No. 28. 0-937073-82-2 (paper), 0-937073-83-0 (cloth)

Lectures on Linear Logic. A. S. Troelstra. Lecture Notes No. 29. 0-937073-77-6 (paper), 0-937073-78-4 (cloth)

A Short Introduction to Modal Logic. Grigori Mints. Lecture Notes No. 30. 0-937073-75-X (paper), 0-937073-76-8 (cloth)

Linguistic Individuals. Almerindo E. Ojeda. Lecture Notes No. 31. 0-937073-84-9 (paper), 0-937073-85-7 (cloth)

Computer Models of American Speech. M. Margaret Withgott and Francine R. Chen. Lecture Notes No. 32. 0-937073-98-9 (paper), 0-937073-97-0 (cloth)

Verbmobil: A Translation System for Face-to-Face Dialog. Martin Kay, Mark Gawron, and Peter Norvig. Lecture Notes No. 33. 0-937073-95-4 (paper), 0-937073-96-2 (cloth)

The Language of First-Order Logic (including the Windows program, Tarski's World). Jon Barwise and John Etchemendy, third edition, revised and expanded. Lecture Notes No. 34. 0-937073-90-3 (paper)

Turing's World. Jon Barwise and John Etchemendy. Lecture Notes No. 35. 1-881526-10-0 (paper)

Syntactic Constraints on Anaphoric Binding. Mary Dalrymple. Lecture Notes No. 36. 1-881526-06-2 (paper), 1-881526-07-0 (cloth)

Situation Theory and Its Applications, Vol. 3. Peter Aczel, David Israel, Yasuhiro Katagiri, and Stanley Peters, editors. Lecture Notes No. 37. 1-881526-08-9 (paper), 1-881526-09-7 (cloth)

Other CSLI Titles Distributed by UCP

Agreement in Natural Language: Approaches, Theories, Descriptions. Michael Barlow and Charles A. Ferguson, editors. 0-937073-02-4 (cloth)

Papers from the Second International Workshop on Japanese Syntax. William J. Poser, editor. 0-937073-38-5 (paper), 0-937073-39-3 (cloth)

The Proceedings of the Seventh West Coast Conference on Formal Linguistics (WCCFL 7). 0-937073-40-7 (paper)

The Proceedings of the Eighth West Coast Conference on Formal Linguistics (WCCFL 8). 0-937073-45-8 (paper)

The Phonology-Syntax Connection. Sharon Inkelas and Draga Zec (Eds.) (co-published with The University of Chicago Press). 0-226-38100-5 (paper), 0-226-38101-3 (cloth)

The Proceedings of the Ninth West Coast Conference on Formal Linguistics (WCCFL 9). 0-937073-64-4 (paper)

Japanese/Korean Linguistics. Hajime Hoji, editor. 0-937073-57-1 (paper), 0-937073-56-3 (cloth)

Experiencer Subjects in South Asian Languages. Manindra K. Verma and K. P. Mohanan, editors. 0-937073-60-1 (paper), 0-937073-61-X (cloth)

Grammatical Relations: A Cross-Theoretical Perspective. Katarzyna Dziwirek, Patrick Farrell, Errapel Mejías Bikandi, editors. 0-937073-63-6 (paper), 0-937073-62-8 (cloth)

The Proceedings of the Tenth West Coast Conference on Formal Linguistics (WCCFL 10). 0-937073-79-2 (paper)

Books Distributed by CSLI

The Proceedings of the Third West Coast Conference on Formal Linguistics (WCCFL 3). 0-937073-44-X (paper)

The Proceedings of the Fourth West Coast Conference on Formal Linguistics (WCCFL 4). 0-937073-43-1 (paper)

The Proceedings of the Fifth West Coast Conference on Formal Linguistics (WCCFL 5). 0-937073-42-3 (paper)

The Proceedings of the Sixth West Coast Conference on Formal Linguistics (WCCFL 6). 0-937073-31-8 (paper)

Hausar Yau Da Kullum: Intermediate and Advanced Lessons in Hausa Language and Culture. William R. Leben, Ahmadu Bello Zaria, Shekarau B. Maikafi, and Lawan Danladi Yalwa. 0-937073-68-7 (paper)

Hausar Yau Da Kullum Workbook. William R. Leben, Ahmadu Bello Zaria, Shekarau B. Maikafi, and Lawan Danladi Yalwa. 0-93703-69-5 (paper)

Ordering Titles Distributed by CSLI

Titles distributed by CSLI may be ordered directly from CSLI Publications, Ventura Hall, Stanford, CA 94305-4115 or by phone (415)723-1712, (415)723-1839. Orders can also be placed by FAX (415)723-0758 or e-mail (pubs@csli.stanford.edu).

All orders must be prepaid by check or Visa or MasterCard (include card name, number, and expiration date). California residents add 8.25% sales tax. For shipping and handling, add $2.50 for first book and $0.75 for each additional book; $1.75 for first report and $0.25 for each additional report.

For overseas shipping, add $4.50 for first book and $2.25 for each additional book; $2.25 for first report and $0.75 for each additional report. All payments must be made in U.S. currency.

Overseas Orders

The University of Chicago Press has offices worldwide which serve the international community.

Canada: David Simpson, 164 Hillsdale Avenue East, Toronto, Ontario M4S 1T5, Canada. Telephone: (416) 484-8296.

Mexico, Central America, South America, and the Caribbean (including Puerto Rico): EDIREP, 5500 Ridge Oak Drive, Austin, Texas 78731 U. S. A. Telephone: (512)451-4464.

United Kingdom, Europe, Middle East, and Africa (except South Africa): International Book Distributors, Ltd., 66 Wood Lane End, Hemel Hempstead HP4 3RG, England. Telephone: 0442 231555. FAX: 0442 55618.

Australia, New Zealand, South Pacific, Eastern Europe, South Africa, and India: The University of Chicago Press, Foreign Sales Manager, 5801 South Ellis Avenue, Chicago, Illinois 60637 U.S.A. Telephone: (312)702-0289. FAX: (312)702-9756.

Japan: Libraries and individuals should place their orders with local booksellers. Booksellers should place orders with our agent: United Publishers Services, Ltd., Kenkyu-sha Building, 9 Kanda Surugadai 2-chome, Chiyoda-ku, Tokyo, Japan. Telephone: (03)291-4541.

China (PRC), Hong Kong, and Southeast Asia: Peter Ho Hing Leung, The America University Press Group, P.O. Box 24279, Aberdeen Post Office, Hong Kong.

Korea and Taiwan (ROC): The American University Press Group, 3-21-18-206 Higashi-Shinagawa, Shinagawa-ku, Tokyo, 140 Japan. Telephone: (813)450-2857. FAX: (81)472-9706.